Praise for *Grace Under Pressure*:

'Very powerful, very moving, and an important contribution to better understanding of a much misunderstood condition' Alastair Campbell

'This is a book about Asperger's Syndrome and a book about running, but it's so much more than that. It's at heart a love story, testament to the power of a parent's fierce devotion to their child. Any parent will see in it something of themselves' Gaby Hinsliff, journalist and author of *Half a Wife*

'Incredibly moving and inspiring. A mother always wants what's best for her daughter, but this mum has to really fight – and run – to get it' Ruth Field, bestselling author of *Run Fat Bitch Run*

About the Author

Sophie Walker has worked as a journalist for Reuters news agency for fifteen years, reporting news around the globe. She has written about oil, trade and politics in Washington and has been foreign correspondent in the UK, travelling to Iraq and Afghanistan with Tony Blair and Gordon Brown.

GRACE
UNDER PRESSURE

Going the distance
as an Aspergers mum

SOPHIE WALKER

piatkus

PIATKUS

First published in Great Britain in 2012 by Piatkus

Some names have been changed to preserve anonymity.

Peterborough City Council		
60000 0000 75430		
Askews & Holts	Oct-2012	
618.928	£13.99	

ISBN 978-0-7499-5826-8

Typeset in Minion by M Rules
Printed and bound in Great Britain by
Clays Ltd St Ives plc

Papers used by Piatkus are from well-managed forests
and other responsible sources.

MIX
Paper from
responsible sources
FSC® C104740

Piatkus
An imprint of
Little, Brown Book Group
100 Victoria Embankment
London EC4Y 0DY

An Hachette UK Company
www.hachette.co.uk

www.piatkus.co.uk

Contents

For my big girl, the grace of my heart and my little girl, who brightens my days. And for my husband, who always said I could.

1

The horror, the horror

Imagine that you have a child whom you love very much. Now imagine that you go to collect this child after work every day. Now imagine that every day when you pick your child up her first words to you are: 'Do I have to clean my teeth tonight?' Regardless of what you say to your child – yes, yes of course, yes, just like last night, yes, because otherwise you'll get sore teeth, yes, you know you do, yes, everyone else does, yes, we've been through this, yes, come on now, don't be silly – your affirmative response will prompt anything from twenty minutes to two hours of negotiating, arguing, shouting, tears, temper tantrums or hysterical meltdown. By the time your child has brushed her teeth, you are both exhausted and swear to each other that it won't be like this any more. The teeth will get brushed, you won't shout, you'll both be friends. You hug and kiss, worn out.

The next day you go to pick up your child and the first thing she asks you is: 'Do I have to clean my teeth tonight?'

This is what evenings with Grace are like, except that her question is: 'Do I have to do my homework tonight?'

To be clear: Grace's teacher does not give her masses of homework. What she does give her amounts to about half an hour on four nights a week. I am glad the school gives her homework. I think it's necessary for her to learn, it's a good discipline and much of it is enjoyable.

But the daily task of getting her to accept that she's got to do it is driving me mad. That sentence doesn't do justice to how it feels. It's not just mad like: arggh, this again. It's mad like proper, ancient, deep-in-the-brain lunacy. It's mad like the dark places where poets and criminals and people in scary films go. It's mad like Sylvia Plath's wild, bald moon and the Joker's rictus grin.

Sometimes I feel like running out of the house even as I'm thinking how much I missed her while I was at work.

Today, to calm myself as Grace raged, I counted up the number of days left on which I have to do this. It's two weeks till the end of term. There won't be any homework next week and most of this week's is done. So really I've probably only got one more night of this. I calculated that so far this school year we have had homework negotiations on 196 nights. No – take off Fridays – that's 156 nights, or 156 hours, if I average out the length of time we reason or row; 6.5 days. So nearly a week of madness.

Put in that context, I've had another fifty-one weeks which are better.

So what am I complaining about?

The conversation about homework is really nothing compared to the process of doing it. Or getting Grace to do it while I supervise simultaneously wrangling two-year-old Betty and cooking the dinner and clearing up, which is usually how it goes.

This is no fun, but it's a lot less no fun for me than it is for Grace.

Grace hates homework with more than your average nine-year-old's passion. She hates it because she knows she'll either understand it with a glance and do it in under five minutes (this applies to story-writing, grammar or spelling exercises and any kind of drawing) or she will not understand it (maths, reading comprehension, any instructions that the teacher hasn't calmly explained several times before Grace brought the worksheets home) and so spend the next hour in a panicky fog of incomprehension.

Tonight it was mainly grammar exercises so we managed, but a set of previously unseen instructions did tip the balance briefly. Grace held her head and rocked back and forth while rolling her eyes, urging herself to understand what she was supposed to be doing. Sometimes when that happens I have to calm her down, or she will start to hit herself. Sometimes I ignore her. And sometimes I tell her off for being silly. Tonight I did all three, and then I shouted. Immediately her level of distress mounted and consequently it took us another ten minutes to calm down, and another five before we could start again.

Sometimes I find myself thinking that Grace will grow out of this. Sometimes I tell myself she'll learn not to do it. Most of the time, I don't know what to think, so I just try to deal with the situation in hand and move on.

One of the hardest things about being a good mum to Grace is knowing when the level of homework distress is related to her having Asperger's Syndrome and when she's just being a stroppy pre-teen.

Grace was formally diagnosed with Asperger's Syndrome only last year, after five years of waiting lists, inconclusive assessments, repeated questioning and a lot of shoulder shrugging. By then, Grace's dad and I had years of rationalising that we suddenly needed to re-examine and recalibrate: from how we reacted to the little idiosyncrasies to how we dealt with odder behaviour, to coping with the bigger things we really worried about. Even now, we're only at the start of figuring out what's AS and what's not (and we don't always agree).

For a long time, we thought Grace's distance and 'otherness' might be a reaction to us divorcing. We put down to eccentricity her fear of dogs and balloons and hand-dryers. (We've since learned that 'Aspies' are extraordinarily sensitive to their surroundings – what we heard as loud noise was really painful to her.) Her inability to read people, or to show curiosity about them, or participate in conversations was, of course, classically autistic and seems so obvious now that I berate myself daily for not realising it sooner and tell myself to be more sensitive in future to her behaviour.

So when Grace greets me at the school gates with a glare and the words, 'I'll kill myself if you make me do piano practice', do I accept that she just has no filter for her sentiments and is anxious that she may not be able to play something new? Or do I tell her off for being rude to me and put it down to a nine-year-old's melodrama?

When she refuses to eat her dinner because I have forgotten about her dislike of houmous (bad middle-class mum!) and put it in the centre of her plate, where it has touched other foods, do I scold her for overreacting and tell her to eat the rest? Or do I calm her down and get her a new plate?

One day, on our way home from school, Grace was railing about the unfairness of being told off by her teacher for lashing out at a classmate (and familiar foe) who was taunting her (again.) In fury, Grace had pulled this girl's hair – and received a whack from her by way of compensation. They were both reprimanded and warned not to do it again. Grace was baffled by this and felt a huge injustice had been done to her.

As she sat in the car shouting that her life wasn't fair I tried to reason with Grace that she shouldn't have touched the girl who was teasing her – no matter how hurtful or annoying. Grace just shouted louder, fists clenched on her lap and the colour rising in her face: 'This was the WORST day of my LIFE.'

At that, I saw red and shouted back: 'For God's sake, Grace, how could you possibly think it's OK to go around pulling people's hair? What planet are you on?'

For a moment, she paused. Then her face crumpled – and she looked like a confused four-year-old again – and she bent her head and sobbed. Loudly. Then more loudly. Then wailed and yelled louder still. In the confined space of the car the amplification of Grace's rage and hurt was overwhelming and unbearable, like an audio bomb had gone off.

Navigating rush-hour traffic I barely saw, I felt panicked and sad. Grace really is on a different planet from the rest of us – it's how Aspies see themselves. A widely used and popular online forum for the autistic and Aspergers community is www.wrongplanet.net. For a child, being on the wrong planet must be even more frightening and confusing. Had I made a terrible, insensitive blunder and compounded her feelings of separateness and worry? How then should I teach her to rein in the kind of behaviour that looked to others to be self-centred and wilful? Was it one or the other or both?

At home I fretted and frowned while Grace played piano (flawlessly) and I cooked.

Over the dinner table we faced each other in tentative silence. Then Grace said: 'Hey, Mummy –' and pulled the silliest face she could imagine. I laughed, and she laughed, and baby Betty cheered and threw food in excitement.

It was a mistake to try to separate bits of my daughter into comprehensible compartments. She is the sum of her parts. She is Grace and she needs patience and understanding and love. Lots of love.

But how could I provide all of that given the state I was in? I was frightened for her, sleepless and worrying and frazzled. I was dizzy with tiredness and knotted with stress. I shouted – all the time. I was entirely incapable of resolving her fears and tantrums with patience and love.

Clearly I had to take myself in hand.

I started by going to the doctor. I told him about Grace and about my high-powered job, which was unravelling. I told him that I couldn't sleep, that I often woke in tears, that I felt hopeless and useless. The words came as a shock to me even as they came out of my mouth. I felt as though I was observing myself from a corner of the room. When did it come to this? How could I have let it get this bad?

I'm not used to failing.

When I was fifteen, my mum came into my bedroom one night to speak to me. I was sitting on the floor in front of the mirror in my wardrobe, trying out a new hairdo. I had pictures of models from *Elle* magazine torn out and stuck to the walls; a collage of film stars and singers patched above my bed; torpedo-like lipsticks Blu-Tacked in formation (a jokey homage to flying ducks) over the sink in the corner, upon which bristled a range of potions.

My mum sat on my bed and addressed me in a tone somewhere between affectionate exasperation and despair. I remember so well the way she held herself tightly and the clipped way she spoke the words under the stress of not losing her temper. She told me that I had a choice to make. I could either sit in my room and listen to pop music and paint my face and fritter my life away. Or I could be a serious person. Study, learn and take on the world. Be somebody. Make something of myself. But I'd have to start now. Because time was wasting.

That sense of time passing and the worry of leaving things undone or not done well enough has been with me ever since. The other thing my mum used to tell me – usually when I'd expressed an idle wish that something would hurry up – was: 'Don't wish your life away.' Lately I had found myself thinking of that again and would be immediately rooted to the spot by panic. I could almost feel a breeze lifting my clothes and rustling my hair: the air, the seconds, the minutes – the achievements I was grasping for – swooshing past me and leaving me behind.

All my life I have run to keep ahead, to keep moving, to dodge failure. But somehow here I was, failing. It had caught up with me just the same.

I was not a good mother. I was not a good employee. I could barely function.

The doctor suggested antidepressants and tutted when I shook my head. 'If it was medicine for your heart, you'd take it,' he told me. But it was for my heart, I wanted to cry. My heart was breaking. For Grace, for me, for the mess I was making. I didn't want pills to make me numb. I wanted to feel the fault lines fracturing my chest and the claggy self-pity which clung to me like reeking mud.

So then I went to see a therapist. I refused to take my business to anyone who I suspected would ask me to lie on a couch and assess my family relationships for the next ten years. I wanted someone who would fix me, fast. I found a man who specialised in cognitive behavioural therapy. He said he could help me retrain my brain and substitute my expectations of failure with hope of success.

At one point not far into the sessions, he said to me: 'Oh boo-hoo, poor you. What are you going to do about it?'

I went back to the doctor and took the prescription for antidepressants.

And I forced myself to keep talking to the therapist.

Eventually, things started to improve. I went whole days without crying. I began to see how self-indulgently bleak I had become. I kept asking myself: 'What are you going to do about it?'

One day I woke and realised I hadn't done any exercise for months. My baby daughter was nearly two. I had lost post-pregnancy pounds mainly through stress. My physical health was as neglected as my mental wellbeing. I was round-shouldered and hollow-eyed and the flesh on my belly white and loose. Before Betty's arrival I used to run – short distances, admittedly – but regularly and with relative ease. Clothes used to look good on me. I used to feel good in my skin.

I got out of bed and went to look for my running kit. After a while I found it: musty, creased and a size too small. I put it on, gritting my teeth against the cling of the fabric to my wobbly thighs and the tight seam of elastic around my waist. I ran down the road and started to feel ill after 200 yards. After five minutes, I wanted to cry and throw myself down in defeat.

I kept going though and finished a small circuit around the local park. The experience was absolutely wretched. Over the next few weeks I tried again, and again. It didn't get any easier. Frustration and nausea marked my efforts. How I had ever run 3 miles was beyond me. It seemed an impossible target: something that only other people did.

A bit like running marathons.

So.

Why not run a marathon instead? I wondered. If I was going to set myself an impossible target, I should at least make it an impressive one. If I was going to go out and wobble and struggle and wheeze, then it would be more heroic to do it in the pursuit of completing 26 miles, rather than a circuit of two swings, a slide and several dollops of dog shit.

When my therapist asked me in our final session what I was going to do next, I answered: 'I'm going to run the London Marathon and I'm going to do it for the National Autistic Society.' He watched me, expressionless, and for a moment I wavered. Was this really wise? Was I falling back into old habits of having to prove myself over and over? Of having to achieve or lie awake worrying about the consequences?

Possibly, but in the process I'd get a lot healthier, I reasoned. I would work off at least some of my anxiety and be calmer and stronger around Grace. I might even do those 3 miles.

At work, I strode over to a friend and announced that I'd decided to run the London Marathon. She looked at me, assessing my cheery smile and slight tremble. 'Good luck,' she said. 'It took me five times before I got a place in the ballot.'

A ballot? I had to hope to be selected? Again, I wavered. Running the marathon had become a Thing very quickly and the prospect of going back to not having something big and scary to do was even bigger and scarier.

I applied for the 2012 London Marathon twice – once

through the ballot and again for a place on the National Autistic Society's team. Then I found a half-marathon that was taking place much sooner and applied for that too. I set up a fundraising page on the internet asking my friends and family to support me in my endeavour to run for the charity that sought to explain and advise about autism and support those affected by it.

Suddenly I was invigorated. I set up a blog (about which I knew nothing technically) and a Twitter feed (ditto). I used too much pink font. But what I lacked in design skills I made up for in energy, invigorated by the belief that after years of desperately trying to do the right thing for Grace, I had finally found a measure of practical support. I sat up late into the night, typing and clicking and formatting, fuelled by the feeling that this – this – would make a difference.

I studied the training plan for the Royal Parks half-marathon and tried to work out how I could build up my twice-weekly not-quite-3-mile run into a 13.1-mile circuit within four months. For a start, it would involve keeping going for more than forty-five minutes: a mysterious and wonderful thing if I could make it happen. I scheduled a training run for the next evening.

All the next day, I watched with delight the rising total on my fundraising page and looked forward to the buoyant pace I would undoubtedly set on my run after work. Alongside the pledges of hard cash, I received several affectionate and encouraging emails, some from the most unexpected sources. I was thrilled that my adventure had moved so many people already.

By the time I got home, a light drizzle had turned into boringly steady rain. Not enough to be a downpour, not enough to be ignorable. I sat and watched the rain drip from the trees and railings outside my house. It was a nice evening otherwise: the air smelled clean and the rush-hour traffic had subsided.

My husband came home grey-faced and tense after a rough day at work. I heard myself suggesting a Chinese takeaway and bottle of wine to cheer him. Result: he perked up immediately, while I was stricken with guilt and a feeling of irresponsibility. As I put down the phone on Man Chui's perky delivery girl (wait time: twenty minutes) the rain stopped abruptly and light emerged from behind the clouds.

I set my alarm for six o'clock the next morning. Being shamed into training for a fundraising race in which I had cajoled my friends and family to stake money was not a good feeling.

A few weeks later, I ran 5 miles in an hour. More experienced runners will groan or smile at this: it's not very far, or very fast. But it was further and faster that I'd done before and I was euphoric.

That day the weather was absolutely gorgeous and I started at a modest pace. For the first fifteen minutes the path took me through the park, alongside the stream and down between the allotments, bursting squares of leafy fecundity. As well as making good progress and not being at all out of breath, I settled on the 'leafy fecundity' phrase for inclusion in my blog later on, and was feeling very pleased with myself when I popped out at the top of the golf course and turned right for the nature reserve.

At this point, the road sloped upwards and went past an uninspiring development of new flats. The combination of gradient and utilitarian boxes cooled my momentum, though alas, not literally, as the sun had emerged and was now toasting me uncomfortably. Still, I made it up the hill without stopping and coasted into the woodland part of the route prepared for five glorious minutes of downhill pace.

The weekend's downpours had turned the dirt track into a boggy cauldron across which I hopped and cursed. Hopping downhill is a lot less energy efficient than running down and by the time the route wound uphill again towards the kissing gate, I was starting to panic. My energy levels and confidence were shot, but not to complete the run would feel like a big failure. I just couldn't figure out how I was going to make it up the hill. At this point, the track narrowed into a shadowy tunnel where thorny trees on either side meshed to blot out the sun. I found myself thinking of the scene in *The Wizard of Oz* where Dorothy is chased through the wood by the scary flying monkeys – oh, for a flying monkey, I wondered wildly. At least then I'd be aloft.

And then – salvation. An elderly hiker was a hundred yards ahead of me, striding along with his stick as I puffed and staggered behind him. Even better, someone else coming the opposite way saluted him and strode towards me with a smile. I was forced to straighten up and smile like everything was fine (although my colour betrayed this) and I summoned the wherewithal – from I know not where – to make it up the hill.

And then it was home free. I had to resort to my iPod and

the same pounding '80s rock song to manage the final fifteen minutes, but by that point I was without shame. Whatever got me to the end. I would have worn my shorts on my head if someone had told me it would give me extra reserves of energy.

When I got home I realised that not only had I run for more than forty-five minutes, but I had done it in an almost entirely physical state, engrossed in what my body was doing. My mind was as clear and rested as my body was sweaty and trembling. I felt happy and, if not strong, then calm and sure of myself.

When I went to pick Grace up from school that afternoon I put my arms around her and held her close.

'What's up, Mummy?' she asked me. 'You look happy.'

2

Welcome to the world, baby Grace

Running through the woods one Saturday morning, six weeks later, I kept returning to the day Grace was born.

At around 5 miles I reached a state of calm, my legs moving easily to the rhythm of my breathing. It was early and quiet except for occasional dog walkers and the birds whirring out of bushes away from me as I passed. Overhead, the trees reached high and laced together against the sun, so that the path led ahead of me in cool, dappled shadow. My stride carried me forward; my thoughts carried me back.

Grace was taken out of me ahead of her due date: a consultant-decreed Caesarean to ensure the safe delivery of an upside-down baby. Instead of being allowed to make her own way into the world – predicted some time around New Year's Day 2002 – Grace found herself suddenly, shockingly airborne, briskly rubbed over, then handed to her similarly bewildered mother two weeks before we had planned to meet.

The first night in hospital she lay beside me in a perspex fish tank, choking in outrage and spluttering viscous bubbles as she sought to expel the amniotic fluid that had not been squeezed out of her by a normal delivery. I was still paralysed from the waist down as the effects of the epidural had not yet worn off, and couldn't reach over to her from my bed. Terrified and impotent, I squeezed a buzzer over and over to summon a nurse for help as Grace gasped for breath. A nurse arrived and, again, Grace was abruptly hoisted, rubbed and inspected. I held her to me for the rest of the night and finally she closed her eyes to her surroundings and drifted away, fists clenched. I watched her eyes move beneath fragile lids and held my breath.

Now, running and remembering, I wondered if this was where her distance from the world began. In the days and weeks that followed, Grace slept on, stubbornly detached from us all. I would hold her in my arms for hours, or peer into her cot after another feed time had passed, or watch her dream surrounded by cushions on the sofa, one tiny pink sock occasionally twitching. Health visitors scurried in and out, telling me off for not nourishing her properly. I would cry with frustration in my attempts to wake her and try to explain to them how hard it was. I would have to tickle her tummy, strip her naked and blow on her, wipe her face with cool flannels and stroke her cheek over and over to try to tempt her to turn and feed. She lost weight and I gained hollows under my eyes. There were dire warnings of drips and hospital visits.

My breath was loud in my ears and I could hear the faint crunch of dry leaves underfoot as I thought back.

Eventually, after several weeks, Grace came round a little. There was jubilation after she finished 4 ounces of milk – in an hour. The rest of her early baby days soon blurred into a recognisable jumble of nappies, routine, broken nights, teething, and I responded to her summonses with weary obedience.

Last year, scientists in Scotland published a study which showed that babies born just one or two weeks early were more likely to develop learning difficulties or conditions such as autism. When I was told nearly ten years ago that Grace would have to be delivered by early elective Caesarean I was secretly relieved. She was my first child and I had lain awake in bed at night, looking at my huge bump and fluttering with panic at the prospect of pushing something so big out of me.

That Saturday morning I ran 11 miles. At the end I wondered how many of them would have been necessary if I had just asked what might happen, instead of signing that consent form.

I have suffered many of those moments in the months since Grace's diagnosis. Thoughts of 'What if?' and 'Why didn't I?' and – the real kick in the stomach – 'How could I not have realised?' circle inside my head and beat in my blood.

For I knew that Grace was different, though somehow I also did not.

She was a sunny toddler, big-eyed and interested in everything around her. She would observe and ponder and smile. I would talk to her – streams of Mummy chatter that carried us both along through the days. Only recently, I realised that

I was carrying us both along because Grace was not responding. At the time it didn't occur to me that a two-year-old could chat back. I thought it was normal to talk for two, to ask the same thing several times and then answer it myself. I heard plenty of mums around me doing the same. I just didn't pick up on the difference in the ages of our children. Then one day, several months ago, standing in the hallway winding a scarf around my neck, I said brightly to baby Betty: 'Let's go out, shall we?' The resounding 'Yes!' from her nearly felled me. She laughed to see the look of surprise on my face and said it over and over again. I laughed with her, but I was as devastated as I was delighted.

As Betty's vocabulary exploded; as she pointed and named and asked question after question after question, I wanted to weep for my baby Grace and my earlier self, swimming unknowingly in that silence.

Why did I not know? There are enough books, tapes, websites. Everywhere there are baby gurus to tell us how our children should be developing. I had the middle-class parent's library: Penelope Leach, Sheila Kitzinger, Miriam Stoppard. I studied Grace minutely, daily, end to end. From the freckle on her thumb to the pin-prick dimples beside her ears, to the tea-leaf birthmark on her leg, I knew her.

And yet, I didn't.

From early on, Grace had an independent, stubborn spirit. She had strong, straight eyebrows, black lashes and hazel eyes that turned topaz in sunlight. With a clear and even gaze she would examine things for ages and refuse all attempts to budge her. Rainy-day walks and trips to the park could be torture as she would have to step in every puddle, with both feet, and observe the ripples. Queuing for the swings in the playground, she would roar with baffled anger and impatience at being made to wait, then switch to profoundly calm enjoyment when her turn came.

At times, her intractability alarmed me. But then I would observe another parent's playground fight or hear the shrieks of another red-faced child in the supermarket. At home, Grace and her father were clearly similar. She was like him, I thought: a clever, obdurate philosopher convinced of her own rightness and certain of her path.

When Grace was two and a half, we all moved to the United States. It was a new take on an old problem: her dad and I were frayed and rowing and wondering if we might be better at being us somewhere else. We took ourselves and Grace out of beaten-down, on-the-up north London and moved to the suburbs of Washington DC: picket fences, flagpoles, yard sales and all. Our new neighbours were a man from the Department of Defense, who had converted his cellar into a safe room full of bottled water and declined to be drawn into conversation, and a smiling salesman and his smiling stay-at-home wife who, smilingly, pointed out to us on day two that we had to park our car facing in the same direction as everyone else's.

Grace loved the flight, loved the house, loved the sandpit and the screen door, behind which she would stand and survey the street and listen to the crickets' endless chirrup. At nursery school, however, her teacher raised an eyebrow and told us: 'She likes to go to Graceland, doesn't she?'

Her father and I thought her solitary habits were a reaction to the move. Grace's pink-cheeked and soft-bodied childminder-cum-Nana had been replaced by a gruff Ghanaian nanny who expressed her devotion through rough hair brushing and nail clipping and stern exhortations to eat well. Her earnest Hackney nursery (report card: 'Today Grace enjoyed expressing her emotional feelings and blowing bubbles') was replaced by a church-like Montessori school where the children wore smart sweaters and had names like Frank and Mary. We thought the Montessori system would suit her independent spirit; in fact, it was possibly the worst choice we could have made. Grace was encouraged to find her own level of often lonely play: counting beans into jars, swooshing water between cylinders, reading and rereading her favourite book (*A Platypus, Probably*). At playtime, when the children dived outside to pedal round and round on tiny red trikes, laughing and careering and shouting, Grace would stand to one side and watch. Or she would spin herself around, arms by her sides, with her eyes looking to the side as if she thought she might catch up with herself if she went fast enough.

We thought she had shut down protectively while she got her bearings.

Around this time, I gave Grace a copy of Disney's *The Little Mermaid* on DVD. In retrospect it feels as though the precise moment should be freeze-framed, blown up, writ large and trumpeted aloud. Sirens should have gone off, the ground should have trembled. People should have clutched each other and turned to watch. For this was a defining moment.

Grace watched the film and was entranced. She watched it again, and again. Very soon we had to set rules about how often and when she could watch it. When she couldn't watch it, she wanted to talk about it, scene by scene. She began to draw mermaids and spot them wherever we went (you'd be amazed how often the symbol occurs once you begin to look). Before very long, Grace could recite huge chunks of the film, word for word.

At Hallowe'en there was only one thing she wanted to be. We obliged, laughingly and just a little awkwardly, telling ourselves it was sweet and she'd be so happy and, anyway, it was just the thing she was into for now. I ordered a mermaid costume from an online party firm. When it arrived it was more Rita Hayworth than Ariel, but the look of delight on Grace's face will stay with me for ever. We have a short film of her wearing the outfit and singing the song 'Part of Your World' from the film. She is two years and ten months old and she is word perfect, despite struggling to get her tongue around some of the vocabulary and clearly not knowing what much of it means. She stands in front of our stripy Crate and Barrel sofa, on a jute rug, by a bookcase and shimmers and wiggles in her green sequinned dress, every action remembered and mimicked in perfect detail. Proudly, she brushes her flowing red wig back from her forehead and, at one point, continues to sing as she picks strands of it off her tongue, to the sounds of muffled parental giggling behind the camera. She is gorgeous and bittersweet as she lilts: 'I want to be where the people are ... wish I could be part of that world.'

Not long afterwards the nursery school informed us that

Grace had failed a hearing test. We got the news in a crisp, impersonal letter, along with a referral to a specialist children's centre for further tests. There were no alarm bells, nor formal warnings. Like so many of the medical responses to Grace in her early years, the tone seemed to be one of: 'It's probably nothing to worry about, but best to get it checked out.'

So we attended our appointment. Standing opposite the building, a Soviet-style concrete square, I had a brief flicker of worried thought: would this be the beginning of something? Grace's still-baby hand was in mine as we waited for the traffic lights to change so that we could cross. I looked down at her fine hair and bare arms and at her profile. She was regarding the cherry blossom on the tree across the street, waiting for me. I tugged her arm gently and she turned and squinted up and we smiled at each other.

Inside the building, a woman explained that Grace would have been expected to respond to various stimuli in the first test, and that this exercise would take place in a more controlled environment to allow no margin for error. Grace was seated in a small booth in front of a grid of switches and lights. She was fitted with huge headphones that sat heavily on her small cheeks. Her expression was blank: from our seats in the corner of the room her father and I could not tell if Grace could hear the voice in her ears asking her to complete various tasks. She seemed passive and accepting of the experience. She was also interested enough to complete the tests accurately this time. There was nothing wrong with her hearing. We went home.

No one suggested anything other than that this was the end of the episode. There was no further discussion, no hint that this might be a clue to something else. It was three years before the next childcare specialist handed me a report card noting that 'Grace has poor attention and listening skills, reduced eye contact and a tendency to hum to herself' as the first clues to the fact that she might have Asperger's Syndrome.

As I write this now, I have Grace's file in front of me. It is a pink binder with multicoloured elastic straps in which I keep all her important stuff. From it spill early drawings, her first birthday cards, school photographs. There is her red medical book, noting her vaccinations and weight gain as a baby. There is *Lily and the Mermaid*, the first book she wrote at the age of five, proudly bound and illustrated. As I thumb through the contents of her file, their nature changes and the sheaves of paper start to look more official.

There are more reports, more headed notepaper. They make for bleak reading. They do not tell of my funny, talented daughter. They do not recount how marvellously she draws and acts and dances. One of them tells me Grace's language skills are at the low end of normal. Another tells me that she can't understand concepts or abstract ideas and interprets questions too literally. Whose daughter is this? My Grace is no dolt. She sparkles and entrances and holds any room in the palm of her hand. Still another report notes that Grace is easily distracted and doesn't greet people correctly or engage in social interaction appropriately, often offering irrelevant information or digressing to talk about her own interests. What I thought was dreamy or artistic or eccentric or childish has been formalised into quite something else.

True, Grace's social skills were definitely off as a small child. She would be invited for playdates and then drift around the friend's house until she found something to which she would devote her entire attention, regardless of what the friend was doing. When little chums came to our house, I would have to direct her in playing together, having once too often discovered the friend cast aside as Grace – usually wearing an astonishing creation – acted out her own invented game. Birthday parties were a nightmare because she was terrified of balloons, having been jolted into traumatised shock when one burst near to her at one of the first she attended. At her own party she remained largely aloof, though clearly happy. At nursery school she made one close friend.

In Washington I started to run. My job was highly stressful, worries about Grace were constant, niggling hooks into my brain, and the atmosphere at home was strained. At first, I went to the gym and ran on the treadmills there. I would turn our jeep down mile after mile of massive boulevard, park in a three-storey holding pen for the giant trucks which seemed to be the obligatory mode of transport in that city and then make my way upstairs to the air-conditioned workout zone. I worked my way from ten minutes without stopping, to twenty, to thirty. But each outing was time-consuming and although the hours away from home were often a relief, the experience was not particularly enjoyable or reinvigorating.

So I took to running outside, starting in small squares

around the grid of our suburban home and gradually making them wider. I would run at six o'clock in the morning to beat the crushing summer heat, wearing the smallest of shorts and vests and praying that no one would see me. Five minutes into my run I would be limp and soaked, entirely reliant on shouty, strident songs on my iPod to drive me forward. In winter, I would put on three layers and wince as I breathed in sub-zero air through my nose instead of my mouth in order not to set my teeth on edge. I ran 3 miles, three times a week.

The months passed.

We moved back to London when Grace was four, our family unit now in pieces. I rented a flat in a pretty yellow house in south London that had bluebells and roses and a foxhole in the front garden. I bought curtains for Grace's room that had castles and princesses and fairies on them. I signed her up for art club and swimming lessons – the latter a huge hit, given her mermaid obsession. Her father moved into a flat on the other side of the village and Grace would trot up and down the hill according to the calendar we had worked out between us.

On days when Grace was not with me, I would run and run and think about her until the thinking wore off. I could still only manage a maximum of forty-five minutes each time – out over the heath and through the park, down avenues of chestnut trees under big skies to the crest of the hill, where the glittering glass of Canary Wharf and the cranes of the Millennium Dome would be spread out below. I would check my mental bruises since the separation and fret about Grace's state of mind.

Walking her to school in the mornings, I had started to notice how difficult it was to talk about normal things with her. Conversation had to be snatched in fragments amid Grace's tumbling stream of consciousness, from rambling stories involving her as a mermaid or the latest adventures of one of her imaginary characters. She had little or no desire to talk about her surroundings or her day ahead. Again, I thought perhaps she was constructing a protective shield, and would try gently to draw her out in order to discover how she was feeling. Sometimes, equally gently, she would smile at me, and continue her tale as though I had not spoken. Other times, she would just raise her voice and talk over me.

I also started to notice that when I dropped her off in the playground she would walk to the line where her class was waiting to go in and elbow herself a place near the front, blank-faced and impervious to her classmates' objections. I came to see her one playtime after a bad row that morning about getting up – a process that seemed to become more and more tortuous – and found her standing to one side, talking to herself and sketching pictures in the air.

And then her teacher raised an eyebrow and said: 'Some of Grace's behaviour is a concern.'

3

The meeting with the man in the suit

On days like this, fury sparks from my fingertips and turns my stomach to ground glass and lacerates my tongue. On days like this, fury makes me clench my teeth until my head hurts. On days like this, I want to grab Grace by the hand and run until everything is far and we are somewhere else.

This is a day when I sat in a room with a man in a suit, and a teacher and a father, and tried to accomplish the impossible task of rendering Grace in simple words, of reaching through the subjective and objective to present her flawed perfection, so that they would see her and understand her and help her.

But it didn't work like that.

First of all, the man in the suit had already decided, in the face of incontrovertible evidence to the contrary, that Grace was doing fine and advancing well in her schoolwork and social setting. This was so that he didn't have to summon extra money for teaching that would be tailored to her needs and for playground support to help her interact. In his picture, the sun always shone, the classroom was a warm friendly place and all were working together to make progress. Thus, he had turned down our request for a 'statement of educational needs'. He tilted his head earnestly as he spoke and distributed a seventeen-point list of criteria, all while assuring us that he abhorred 'box-ticking mentality'.

Also in the room was the teacher, who in order to change the man's mind and secure necessary extra help (and funds) had compiled a picture of Grace and her needs that was heart-breaking and hair-raising. In this picture, Grace was a growling, pacing misanthrope. Violence was never far from the surface, schoolwork was all but irrelevant and tears and chaos reigned. The teacher smiled sympathetically and twisted her hands.

Watching and occasionally asking questions was the father. His Grace was intense but loving, bright and talented, prone to occasional eccentricities and often misunderstood. This man's eyes flashed with impatience as he followed the proceedings.

And me? I danced among them, hopping and cajoling and mediating. I wondered who was right. I wondered why my version of her tallied with none of the above. I wondered how much of the situation was my fault and whether I was doing enough to fix it. I wondered what to do for the best. I wondered if I was doing things wrong.

And I wondered why no one was really talking about Grace and what on earth I could do about it.

So I nursed my rage and I ran as I wondered how much more of this there was.

The comments from Grace's reception teacher had sparked the start of a long process of observation and treatment and deduction, a conveyor belt of doctors and childcare experts and therapists who never seemed quite able to draw a conclusion. No one, it seemed, could tell us precisely what was wrong. Rather, they could list lots of things that were not right. They seemed entirely unable – and unwilling – to diagnose the source of Grace's idiosyncrasies. Whether that was to do with Grace's age or their limited resources, I couldn't tell. But we all trundled along the travelator together anyway, looking at her and wondering and conferring.

Her reception teacher warned: 'What's accepted now will start to look more eccentric as she gets older and could make her the target of bullying.' Suggesting a referral to the local children's services unit, she added: 'The difficulty she is having with maths because of the conceptual language it uses is only going to get worse if we don't find a way to help her.'

But finding a way to help her was like looking for the door out of a glass maze. A lengthy analysis by the community paediatrician reeled off a list of Grace-isms with which by now we were all familiar, then tiptoed around words like 'learning disabilities' and 'Asperger's Syndrome' and rushed to conclude that it was too early to conclude anything and that 'communication skills' classes would help. Grace was put on a waiting list for said classes and referred to a speech therapist who got her age wrong and pegged all her developmental conclusions askew.

The school special needs unit kicked in: Grace had 'circle time' at school where she and some of her classmates who needed extra help discussed social behaviour. She would come home and tell me matter-of-factly that the group had been talking about X again, a very naughty boy who had no friends and would run wild through the playground. I told myself at least she wasn't naughty, or wild.

The teachers at her school figured her out and she seemed, if not exactly to be making progress, to have reached a kind of equilibrium. She was fantastic at some subjects, at a total loss to understand others. We were still on that waiting list.

At that point, we moved to the other side of London, tracing the Northern Line up and up and up. Now eight-year-old Grace had a baby sister, stepbrothers and a stepfather. She loved her new siblings and established an uneasy peace with my new husband.

Then she started a new school, where everything her reception teacher had predicted came true. Grace spent that year being bullied, fighting and railing and being sent out of class when she rose to the bait of classmates who were fascinated by her weirdness and potential for combustion. Maths became a foreign language and the introduction of comprehension exercises poured poison into the pool of her peaceful reading.

I became a regular visitor to her classroom, both to ask for support and to check what homework had been set when Grace claimed to have none. Then I started going to see her headteacher as regularly. She would express surprise when I named the bully ringleaders and tell me they were good kids. Year 3 was always a difficult one, she'd say.

Then one day, I received a phone call from the special needs co-ordinator asking me to come in and discuss Grace. Surrounded – literally: they would encircle her – and tormented even before she'd sat down to have breakfast, Grace had gone for one of her classmates in morning club with a toast knife. There was a pause at the other end of the line after this news was disclosed, in order for me to rush in with shocked apologies.

I said: 'I'm not surprised. She's at the end of her tether and the school has given her no support.'

The special needs co-ordinator replied: 'Well, she brings it on herself.'

Grace had not touched or wounded this child. She had jumped to her feet yelling and waving the knife over her head like an Amazon. I am almost entirely sure that her anger was real and channelled into playing one of the (angry and hurt) characters in her head. The idea of actually slicing and dicing the boy concerned, along with, perhaps, a special needs co-ordinator who could say that a bullied child brought it on herself, belonged entirely to me and I had never communicated either wish to Grace.

That same week, I got a letter postmarked south London to tell me that Grace had a place in the communication classes to which she had been referred now nearly three years previously. Standing in the kitchen with the letter in my hand, I laughed aloud in disbelief and rang the doctor who had written it to explain our current situation. She was appalled and embarrassed and within two days I had received a copy of a second letter from her in which she asked colleagues in our new borough to see Grace as quickly as possible. Their response, several weeks later, was that they were too busy and she'd be put on a waiting list.

While we waited, I wrote an official letter to the school asking to see their anti-bullying policy (after a website for parents advised me that the school would have to keep this as part of their records for the next government inspection) and calling for a meeting with the parents of Grace's persecutors. This had the effect of lobbing a hand grenade into the school office. The school dealt with the bullies and assigned Grace extra help in class. It wasn't enough, but it was a start. She walked a little taller in the mornings.

Six months later, she was called in for a full assessment by the local children's services unit. Two months after that we had an answer.

I had thought Grace's diagnosis would bring certainty. But when I received the phone call I found instead that it threw everything into question. The doctor on the other end of the line asked me if I could come in to discuss the test results. I said yes, of course, and then hastily, bluntly, asked what it was, what conclusion had they reached? The doctor faltered. I rushed in again, the weight of five years' not knowing suddenly too much to bear for another few days. Sounding deeply uncomfortable, the doctor then said: 'Yes, it's an ASD diagnosis.' There were a few more short exchanges, about which I remember nothing, and she rang off.

ASD. I had no idea what she meant. As far as I knew, the tests had been to find out whether Grace had Asperger's Syndrome. The affirmative in the doctor's response left me entirely at sea. So did Grace have Aspergers? Or something else? Was this a relief or a disaster? I stumbled through the rest of the afternoon with Grace and Betty, replaying the conversation in my head until I could get to my computer in private.

Eventually, I got to Google and Wikipedia, which told me that ASD meant autism spectrum disorder, and that it was so termed to encompass the wide range of associated psychological conditions characterised by abnormalities of social interactions and communication, as well as restricted interests and repetitive behaviour.

The meeting with the doctor (chastened by her superior and embarrassed for having told me the result over the phone) and the team of assessors, psychiatrists and speech therapists, revealed that within the ASD diagnosis, Grace had, more specifically, Asperger's Syndrome, with a side order of ADHD – Attention Deficit Hyperactivity Disorder – for good measure.

As I write this chapter I'm grounded from running for a while. I have a virus that makes me feel off-balance, dizzy and out of kilter. The doctor says my inner ear is at fault. I forced myself through 10 miles on Sunday, driven by guilt at not doing it on Saturday when I felt unwell, only to end up queasy and reeling back at my front door. (I completed the run though, and did it faster than the last time.) Now I must be still for a while and take some pills.

But the feeling is not new. Trying to get a fix on how Grace is, or is about to react, often feels like a balancing act: as though I'm tiptoeing along the beam of a ship, braced for the next pitch and yaw, or clutching a spinning compass between two opposing forces.

Many months have passed since the diagnosis and most of the time I'm still at sea. Afloat, yes, and paddling hard: making progress most certainly, but never quite sure where the horizon is. And then there are the regular tidal waves that turn me over and leave me disorientated – like when people say to me they don't think there's much wrong with Grace. 'She's eccentric, charming and interesting,' they tell me. 'Surely that's all it is?' Or they say: 'Oh, my kid does that all the time!' Others declare: 'It's just the age.'

I don't know what to say when this happens. My first reaction is always the same, a lurch of distress in my stomach and taste of panic in my mouth. Am I wrong, then? Are the doctors wrong? Have I condemned Grace by labelling her? Or is this where the spectrum comes in? Is everyone on this spectrum? Are there days when Grace is closer to 'normal' on the spectrum? Just how broad is this bloody thing?

And I feel embarrassed, and I feel guilty as I try to explain that no, Grace has AS, and this is how it manifests itself. What, really, is the point of pigeonholing her if observers see nothing wrong? Do *I* need this more than Grace? Because, by God, if she's not autistic, then she's often a brat and I, by extension, am a bad mother.

To the parents who say their kids enjoy inventing stories too, should I just smile and nod? Or should I tell them that when Grace tells stories, all the rest must stop – and for hours. Should I tell them how last weekend, as her step-brothers played with their robots on the sitting-room carpet, she knelt on all fours across their toys so that she could continue to recite into their faces the ongoing chapter when they got bored?

To the relatives who say, she's just a kid, it's normal when she argues, it's the age, should I just smile and nod? Or should I recount the number of aggressive 'No!'s I get in any given twenty-four hours, from asking her to get up, to asking her to get washed, to get dressed, to leave the house, to go home again, to switch the TV off, to eat her tea, to clean her teeth . . . on and on and on?

To the friends who say, oh their son is totally obsessive too, and won't stop thinking or talking about dinosaurs, or trucks, or planets or whatever, should I just smile and nod? Or should I mention that Grace's mermaid obsession has so far lasted six years? Or that her obsession with Monster High (a collection of freakish and coolly eccentric school kids) means that she draws monsters on every scrap of paper from morning till night? Or that she plays alone every day because she will only play her own Phantom Manor game and no other?

Maybe I need her to be autistic because it's the only answer I've got. The rest is dizzying, and there are no pills for it.

4

I can't help it

It's a small piece of paper. A bit crumpled around the edges. Beige. The handwriting is careful: sloping letters linked by curls at the bottom of each one, done with the care of a child just learning to join them up. Looking at them, you can imagine the tip of a tongue protruding, as the author presses down with the brown felt-tip pen, leaning a little to the right. It would be perfect, but that the exclamation mark has been smudged.

Grace brings it to me in the kitchen of our home. She is white-faced. She holds it out to me and tells me that she has just found it in her school bag. I watch a torrent of emotions chase across her features. She laughs, then frowns. As she turns to me, she is angry, uncertain, disbelieving. I read the note and look up at her and open my mouth to speak.

Then: fury. Flinging herself at me with a howl of pain, she snatches the note from me and tries to pull it to shreds while rushing back across to the bin on the other side of the room.

I run after her and turn her to me, grabbing for the note, hating it but wanting it and needing to preserve it, thinking fast: I have to show this to the school tomorrow, she mustn't destroy it.

My daughter's face is a mask of anguish. I hold her to me. She is hot, raging, sobbing. She smells of fresh laundry and school and hormones and pain. She recounts another huge row at school, the one with the horrible child, the one that got worse and worse until she lashed out. Her voice is muffled: she speaks into my chest, hiding her face in hurt and anger while she tells me how she stamped on his foot and shouted in his face.

Then we have the conversation. The one we both hate, and know by heart.

I tell her that I love her, and will do everything I can to help her, and that I know how hard this is. Then I tell her that as soon as she touches or hurts someone, then no matter what they have done, no matter how they hurt her feelings, no matter that they laughed, or poked, or whispered with others and narrowed their eyes – no matter any of this – it's game over when she hits them.

She breaks away from me and screams and stamps her feet and shouts at me. 'They're stupid, they're horrible, they've all got it in for me.'

'Listen,' I tell her. 'We all have jobs to do. Mine is to look after you and to sort this out, to talk to the school and make sure they fix this. Their job is to stop the bullies and to protect you in class. You have a job to do too,' I tell her. 'Your job is to count to ten and walk away. You have to try.'

'I can't help it,' she throws back at me. She is calmer now, but still red in the face. Her hair stands out from her face in teary, furious knots. 'I've got A-A-Aspergers –' and she is sobbing again.

For a moment neither of us says anything.

My daughter looks at me. 'What is the point of me,' she says flatly.

I force a smile and tickle her cheek and pull her to me. I tell her all the wonderful, marvellous things that are the point of her. I fold her in a warm hug, but inside I shiver.

Later that evening, she comes down from her bedroom. I have just finished writing a long letter to her headteacher – using as a template the last one I wrote to her, so optimistic that it could all be sorted out – and I am sitting on the sofa listlessly, watching a mediocre film.

Grace appears in the doorway in pink rumpled pyjamas, the eye mask she needs to wear pushed up on to her forehead. She looks soft and tender and very, very young. She says to me: 'I've been thinking, and they're right. I am mean. I shout at people. I wish I wasn't here.'

I think of the run I failed to get up and do this morning because it was raining. I think of the strength-training session I failed to do last week because it meant doing boring sit-ups on the sitting-room carpet rather than the glory of notching up a certain number of miles to feel proud of. I remember what the point of it all is, and I am heartbroken to have been given this kind of reminder. I am frightened for her, and I am frightened that I can't fix this for her.

We curl up on the sofa and eat sweets and eventually start

to giggle occasionally at the silly film. For a blissful while we are just us two, mum and daughter, and she is just a nine-year-old who can't quite mask a fleeting smirk when I say that yes, OK, she can stay up a bit later. I would give anything for it to be just this, and only this.

When I initially told Grace about her diagnosis her reaction was one of relief. I was very lucky. Staggering through a form of words that I had not sufficiently rehearsed, I realised, as I told her, that I wasn't well enough prepared to deal with an adverse reaction. I barely understood what I was telling her myself, and I hadn't done very much research. Sure, the phalanx of experts who finally labelled her had given me a list of suggested reading matter that I rushed home to order online. But when it arrived, I could barely look at it. I felt as though I had asked for a supportive hug and been instead directed to a man in a white coat with a clipboard. My recommended reading was a pile of textbooks with abstract cover designs, printed by specialist publishers. They terrified me. The first chapter of one of them intoned: 'How to introduce people with autism to their disability.' I didn't want an MA in autism; I wanted to help my child comprehend and acknowledge who she was.

But Grace was there before me. She listened carefully as I stumbled through my speech. At first, her face bore a tight, anxious expression that I could see her attempting to flatten into carelessness. Then she brightened. 'So I'm like this because I can't help it?' she asked. 'All the things I get wrong are because I've got Asperger's Syndrome?'

I hesitated, with the sensation of having one foot above a landmine. 'Well, it's not really about the things you get wrong,' I told her. 'It means there are some things that you find more difficult because of having Aspergers and that you are brilliant at some other things because of it – like your drawing and your drama and your stories. And now that we know, we can figure out how to help you get better at the tough stuff.'

It was an absolutely terrifying conversation – just writing about it now makes the palms of my hands sweat. All parents bear responsibility for how their child will turn out, of course, but mostly, they get several years to tinker and tweak and adapt. I felt as though I was forging Grace's identity and self-esteem in the turn of a few clumsy, ill-researched sentences. I was so scared that if I got this bit wrong, she would seize on the negatives of her diagnosis and define herself by them.

But, thank God, she was twinkling at me now. 'Does this mean I'm special?' she asked. 'Yes,' I answered fervently. 'Yes, it does.'

We sat together on the sitting-room carpet and talked some more. Grace was very anxious that people at school should understand why she was different, and often, in their eyes, difficult to be around. I asked her if she wanted to tell them. 'Yes,' she answered. 'Yes, please.' It was a year after she had started her new school: a year of misunderstandings, quarrels, meltdowns and, at its worst, co-ordinated bullying from children who had spotted her as an eccentric and an easy target. Grace wanted her peers to understand and forgive her and like her and, in so doing, allow her to understand and forgive and like herself.

So Grace went to school and did a presentation to her class about having Asperger's Syndrome. No announcement was ever so well prepared: no government strategy, corporate policy, scientific discovery, celebrity PR. I talked to her teacher, bought more books and shared them with her. I listened to Grace's suggestions and made some of my own. I lay in bed at night trying to anticipate any questions she might be asked by her classmates.

On the day of the project, Grace did not want me to go into school with her. So I went to work and watched my computer screen with blank eyes as I inwardly fretted.

It went well. Her teacher told me afterwards that watching her pupils' expressions she could see the penny drop. Grace told me of individual reactions: the sweet, soft-hearted playmate who burst into tears when remembering a day Grace had annoyed her; the ferociously bright, competitive chum who stoutly declared that Grace was a good friend regardless; the boys at the back of the class whose eyes slid away as they remembered clashes in the playground.

Grace came home with a spring in her step, her shoulders relaxed.

The next day, a child who had been absent for her presentation confronted Grace at playtime with the words: 'I know you don't have Aspergers. You just made it up. There's no such thing.'

Grace was humiliated and furious and upset. I was floored again by the brutality of the under-elevens. And still, we had absolutely no clue just how much more of this she would have to endure.

In the meantime, she kept trying to make friends.

I invited her friend M to come for a sleepover. It was Grace's first sleepover and she was very excited. Together the girls unpacked M's overnight bag and, between them, negotiated who would have which bed (with only a little input from me). I cooked lasagne, after checking it was also M's favourite food, and lined up chocolate mousse for pudding.

The two girls sat at the table. Grace ate with gusto, pausing now and again to look up and grin at her friend and remind her: 'You're sleeping with me tonight!' M sat opposite, curled on her chair like a mermaid, knees underneath her. She picked daintily at her food and, smilingly polite, told me how tasty it was. We were going on holiday in a few days and she was curious to find out more. 'When you go on holiday, where will you be staying? Is it an apartment? Will you be self-catering?'

Grace looked at her blankly and shrugged. 'It's a house. Come on, we're watching a film after.'

My heart was in my mouth throughout the conversation. Observing Grace navigate the minefields of early friendship and social interaction had me on pins: it was like watching nuclear diplomacy. My mind went back to the conclusions drawn by the stream of assessors we had seen. They told us Grace had poor communication and comprehension skills, an inability to empathise, delayed development.

But Grace is far, far more complex than the sum of her assessments. She fully understands how people feel – she feels the same way herself. She worries about getting it wrong. She worries about people not liking her. She frets about being popular. She is desperate to have her own best friend, the way most other girls in her class do. She just can't read people's moods in the moment or understand why they might behave in a certain way when they're with her; she cannot comprehend the impact that her actions might have on the way insiders relate to her. She is not an emotionless android. She is not Rain Man. I've lost count of the number of times she has thrown herself into my arms, weeping and shouting, 'I feel horrible!' when she realises that, yet again, she has caused hurt or offence.

By now, the girls were sitting on the sofa watching their film. We had created a home-cinema environment: the curtains were closed, the lights were out and Grace and M were munching brownies in the dark and watching the characters find themselves in a casino. M turned to Grace and said: 'Which would you rather go to? Las Vegas or Los Angeles? Los Angeles has Hollywood, but Las Vegas is so pretty with all those lights. Do you know about gambling?'

Grace barely glanced at her, and for a moment I wondered if she had tuned her out to watch the film. Then she got up and drifted over to the other side of the room where she started to dance and sing to herself. M watched for a moment, then turned back to the movie. It was impossible to tell what she was thinking. I wanted to say to her, 'Grace isn't being rude – she just doesn't know the right answer.'

Thinking about this, I was suddenly twelve again and in the bedroom of my school friend Tracy Fleming. I had butterflies in my stomach and the sure knowledge that if I didn't stay on my toes, I'd be toast. Tracy fired questions at me and watched me as closely as a cat. I knew that the trick was to get the answers right, but not so right that Tracy was wrong, and not so wrong that I looked like a loser. Most of the questions would be about just how long I had liked Duran Duran, which songs I knew the words to and which member of the band I fancied. The answers (I thought) were: not as long as she had, none of the ones she liked, except maybe one and anyone, as long as it wasn't John Taylor. I failed. (I could not dissemble about John Taylor.) Tracy's flashing displeasure followed me up the hill as I trailed home and I braced myself for her mocking laughter at school the next day.

I digress, but only a little. M was far kinder than Tracy ever was. But making and keeping friends requires a particular alchemy that we all – bar a few very lucky ones – struggle to perfect. Don't we? I watched Grace and wondered.

The next morning, M's mum arrived to collect her, bringing along her younger sister S, a pert child who fizzed with curiosity. She skipped into the room where Grace, Betty and M were playing. At that moment, Betty squawked at Grace for handling a favourite toy and S laughed and exclaimed: 'She doesn't like you, does she?' at which Grace burst into tears. My reaction was pure instinct – I was across the room in seconds, ferocious and firing at S that that was a nasty thing to say, while cupping Grace under the chin to bring her eyes to mine. 'She didn't mean it, it's not true,' I told her. Grace hiccupped and looked uncertainly back at me. I could see her wondering. Meanwhile, S was round-eyed, frightened and in tears. I apologised to her mum, who was very nice about it. There followed some slightly awkward conversation. I was mortified. How was I supposed to help Grace steer through social situations when I was still crashing around like this?

The next day, I texted M's mum to check in and test the water. She told me to stop worrying and that M had had a great time. Grace was invited to stay the night at their house another time. I wondered whether my nerves could stand it. And what kind of music M's mum liked.

I wonder sometimes if Grace's fragility is inherited from me rather than her diagnosis; whether I am the culprit for the blue vein of vulnerability she displays so clearly beneath her skin. I am running and running now, three or four times a week – sometimes whooping through the nature reserve before daybreak, overloaded with adrenaline and high on being alone to see the cirrus clouds above turn apricot and lavender with the dawn. Other times, it's still a weary slog. It is helping me by framing my days, giving me purpose, letting me work off my worries instead of numbing them with pharmaceuticals.

But still, there are days when emotional overload hits and my systems crash. There are days when I find it so hard to bear the travails of my daughter that the smallest kindness can cause me to leak tears and fumble for a tissue. I love my daughter so much that it can render me incapable and thick-headed.

On one such day I waved her off on a three-day school trip and was so apprehensive for her that I could feel the old fault lines cracking along my heart.

I prepared so well in advance. I washed and ironed and packed and bought little treats and smiled and reassured and giggled along with her in excited anticipation. I tucked a letter to her inside her bag, along with contraband sweeties. In the morning, I brushed her hair and kissed her cheek and stood shivering beside her in the shadow of the school coach for twenty minutes, so early were we.

She is tall, my girl. Slim and elegant, she stands head and shoulders above her classmates. She holds herself well – may she never adopt the embarrassed hunch of long girls waiting for a short world to catch up – and that morning, in the churning crowd of excited classmates, she bent her head again and again to hear what was being said around her, exposing the vulnerable nape of her neck in a way that made my stomach tighten. A friend bounced up to her side and asked if they could sit together. Grace said yes, so long as she could have the window. It was agreed. Then – suddenly – the teachers were all there and it was a scramble to get on the bus. I hugged her and smiled and watched as she got on the coach and discovered that her friend had changed her mind and wanted to sit with someone else. Through the tinted windows of the coach I couldn't make out Grace's expression, but could see only a solitary silhouette waving alongside the rows of excited couples on either side of her.

I blew kisses and mimed hugs and mouthed: 'Never mind. It's OK,' and forced a bright smile as the teacher went to sit with her instead. The coach pulled off and I turned away in grief.

This is ridiculous, I told myself. I know this is ridiculous.

She will be caught up in the events of the next three days at the outdoors activity centre and she will come home with long, rambling tales and an unused toothbrush and mud on the knees of all her trousers.

If only she could come home with a chum, a little soulmate to understand her and hold her hand and be trusted with her heart. If only I could help her mend that chink in her understanding, help her to conceal that vulnerability that brings the bullies, sniffing blood, and distances potential friends or makes the 'good' kids lash out in exasperation too.

In despair one evening, I posted a plea for help on a parenting website, asking how I could protect Grace from the seemingly endless bullying and help her construct more robust friendships. The replies flooded in from parents of children with Aspergers or autism. Many offered practical advice about handling the school, telling me precisely what I needed to ask for, such as written assurances about future strategies. Others offered contact details for national bodies such as BeatBullying and the Children's Rights Alliance and told me to keep a diary. Others yet told me to ring the police and change school as quickly as I could. Some shared horrific experiences.

I read late into the night, my computer screen bright in the darkened house, of emotionally damaged children who had been mentally abused and physically hurt: in one case, a broken nose which the school in question attributed to 'perceived' bullying, so they wouldn't have to acknowledge it. The mother of that child told me her son had had a nervous breakdown at the age of fifteen as a direct result of the abuse he had suffered continuously in school. The psychologist who assessed him described his experience as that of a civilian in a war zone.

One voice offered a particularly clear assessment of the differences that were at the root of such difficulty and upset. She introduced herself as Ann Memmott, an adviser on autism conditions who is, herself, on the autism spectrum. Listening to her sum up the hurdles Grace faced in social situations, I was both grateful for her understanding and impressed by her cool self-knowledge.

As Ann outlined the problems both she and my daughter experienced, one aspect in particular struck me hard as a recurring theme in the stories of difficulty that Grace carried home from school. Most pupils, Ann said, will understand that someone can be sarcastic in a funny way as a friendly joke. But autistic people don't get it because they can't see the body language or the tone of voice that accompanies it and explains the joke.

'So we get upset at what sounds like an attack, which then makes the group angry at us,' she told me. 'Compounding that difficulty,' she added, 'is the inability to read the body language of friends that says, "Join my circle" or, "It's your time to talk now" or, "You need to shut up for a while" or, "We play this game my way." So we make continual blunders,' Ann explained. 'Groups get angry with us again.'

Hearing this is painful beyond words. Realising again how hard Grace must find her days in this environment, I am amazed that she is able to leave the house in the mornings. Particularly when I hear from another parent how her daughter finally snapped after enduring bullying for years at primary school.

Following online signposts and tips from the feedback I received, I joined the National Autistic Society's Facebook page and was befriended by Nic, forty-one, mother of eleven-year-old Sophie, who also has Asperger's Syndrome. We swapped photographs of our children and sent each other cheering messages. Then one night, we talked on the phone, Nic's soft Rochdale accent reminding me of my grandmother. It made me want to reach down the line and hug her. From opposite ends of the country, we talked about our daughters, tutting and laughing at their many similarities and, in hushed moments – I was close to tears several times while Nic recounted her story – feeling each other's hurt.

Nic told me that Sophie used to be physically sick in the mornings because she didn't want to go to school. Then one day, she walked home while Nic was at work and texted her to say: 'Please don't ever make me go back.'

Like Grace, Sophie was a target for bullies because she too found herself constantly on the edge of things, unable to interpret social cues. Unlike Grace, however, she would not retaliate – terrified of breaking any school rules – and, instead, soaked up the abuse until she got home to safety, when the tears and meltdowns would start.

'She would say, "Why am I like this? Why am I so stupid? I wish I was dead,"' Nic told me. 'I remember going in to the headteacher's office in tears – it was breaking my heart – to be told that it was just girls being girls and she had to toughen up.'

At that point, the family removed Sophie from the school. She has since made a successful transition to secondary school but, concludes Nic: 'It's taken a long time for her self-esteem to come back. She still looks in the mirror and thinks she's fat and ugly.'

I am very worried about Grace's self-esteem. She has been referred to a local counsellor, whom I bombard with phone calls and emails when, yet again, we are told we are on a waiting list to be seen. I ask for a meeting at the school to discuss precisely what anti-bullying measures they plan to introduce. I write a formal letter to the headteacher and copy it to the local council's education welfare team – an action that so upsets the headteacher she cannot bring herself to talk to me when I phone and I end up having to soothe her distress too. I email and phone the educational psychologist who was last to see Grace to ask how quickly, precisely, she can start the social-skills classes with her that she has so strongly recommended.

I don't think Grace regards her school as a war zone, quite. She has good days, when she will come bouncing out telling me with cheeky one-upmanship that they had peach crumble for pudding at lunchtime (this is my cue to shake my fist in mock jealousy and swear that I will come in one day and steal some for myself). Or when she tumbles out of after-school club with her stepbrothers on a Thursday – their day for coming to stay with us – and they are all laughing over something that happened and poking each other in mischief.

But then just when we've all relaxed, someone will lob

another hand grenade into her life, into our home, in the form of a note in her school bag. Or say something to her that she finds so humiliating that she goes sleepless for days. Or pick a mindless quarrel that leaves her so bemused and distraught that we have to spend hours unpicking the event to show her how unfounded it was.

One night, exhausted from going around and around an incident with Grace, explaining and soothing again and again, I have to remind myself of Ann's explanation as to why my daughter is so very sensitive: 'Our brains tend to work on the principle that there's one correct answer and it's either perfect, or it's not. If someone is criticising us, it means there is something wrong. If there is something wrong, we've made an error. I find that my brain hits every panic button it has if I'm criticised,' Ann told me. That intense fear and low confidence is often a reason why autistic children live elsewhere in their minds. 'It was the only way to get through each day,' Ann said.

I thought this would get easier. Instead, I'm just getting used to how hard it is.

One Friday night, Grace cried and cried as she recounted the latest incident of classroom teasing. The following Sunday night, having steered her through an anxious weekend and hours of impenetrable homework, I cried and cried as I sat upright in bed in the darkness, unable to sleep for worrying about her. On Monday morning, as we perched knee to knee on tiny chairs in a classroom, Grace's teacher blinked back tears as she apologised for the way she had handled the incident.

It felt like Wonderland, as though, like Alice, we were all bobbing about in a sea of our own tears; struggling through the brine in a crazily distorted landscape and confronted with endless unsolvable riddles.

When the incident in question occurred, Grace's class had been doing computer work, sorting through photographs of their recent school trip and writing up their reports. One of the pictures showed Grace in an ungainly pose, snapped with an expression that rendered her ugly. Observing her discomfort, a classmate gleefully decided to download the photograph as a screensaver. Grace shrieked and slapped her. The classmate slapped her back. Grace burst into tears, drawing the amused attention of a second pupil, while a third printed off the photograph and started waving it about. At this point Grace bolted out of the class, hurt, embarrassed and furious and entirely unable to process the experience.

Grace was volatile all that weekend: in need of soothing routine, yet fretfully chafing at any constraints. In the car on the way to her drama club on Saturday afternoon, she picked up the thread of her story again, and told me how she had tiptoed back into the class and told the teacher what had happened, confessing to her own part in shouting and hitting. The teacher warned the class that anyone talking from then on would miss playtime on Monday. Shortly afterwards, Grace told her neighbour that she liked her drawing. The teacher promptly banned her from Monday play.

Grace reached the conclusion of her story and once again I found myself sitting in the car with her – so many of these scenes involve us sitting in the car – trying to staunch her great, gusty sobs and trying, again, to persuade her every-thing would be all right. I swore to her that she'd get her playtime back. I swore to her that I would take her to school and not leave until I had rebuilt it as a safe place for her. It felt like being confronted by a massive hill at mile eight, won-dering how I would keep going.

And so it was that I went to school with Grace that Monday morning, feigning light-heartedness as we walked there, while inwardly boiling with anger and questions. I had anticipated another long wait in the school office, sitting on the grey felt chairs and reading for the hundredth time on the wall oppo-site the laminated school rules about being nice to each other, while beside me the gluey liquid of the ceramic water feature trickled and plopped. I expected faintly defensive staff and a subtly different version of events. Instead, I was greeted promptly by Grace's teacher and the school's special needs co-ordinator and whisked into an empty classroom where they both hastened to apologise and reassure and tell me the inci-dent had been dealt with. It was clear that both had discussed what happened and felt bad about not having dealt with it better. Grace's teacher paused several times to swallow hard and control the glistening of tears as she told me how fond she was of my daughter and how bright and funny she was. At the end, I stood up and shook hands and left.

It was singularly depressing; unutterably wearying. I know that they feel they are doing their best: Grace now has play-ground buddies and a daily diary, so that she can talk through her feelings; her teacher makes a point of resolving any inci-dents as soon as they happen, so that Grace doesn't have to take her anxieties home. There is progress. The thing is, I am still not sure that they understand *why* it keeps happening, and until they do, I am sure it will keep happening.

Why is there no training for my daughter's teachers? What is the point of a policy of integration if there is no understanding of what we are trying to integrate – no appreciation of the vulnerabilities inherent in Grace's different brain design? I keep remembering Ann's description of the process and it makes me shiver. Putting children who are on the autistic spectrum into a mainstream school that doesn't know what it's dealing with is, she says, 'like putting a Ming vase in the middle of a rugby scrum and hoping that all will go well'.

5

This is me, and I am not Rain Man

So we had a diagnosis. With the diagnosis came a label.

For a long time afterwards in that first year after being told, I felt as though the doctors had slapped a sticker on Grace – 'Fragile, This Way Up' – and left me to stagger off with her, with no destination and no map.

Immediately after the initial shock wore off, I hoped that naming Grace's idiosyncrasy – awarding her the title of a person with Asperger's Syndrome – would present us with some allies, open some doors. Instead, it became evident pretty quickly that we were on our own. Wrestling with the local education authority, we discovered that the label alone wasn't enough to get Grace extra help at school. And, having talked to her classmates in a bid to foster understanding, Grace found that before long things were back to normal in the playground, her new label now just fresh ammunition. Halfway through yet another conversation with me about

Grace's problems at school, her headteacher leaned forward and said earnestly to me: 'The problem is, Grace's disability isn't physical. She looks normal. And that makes it difficult for the other children to understand.'

At this point I started to wonder what it was, really, that this diagnosis could give us. We had travelled along this route because we kept being told that Grace was having difficulties because she was different and that we had to find out why. But now that we had found out why, the people who diagnosed her had moved on to the next interesting case, while the people who had said she was having difficulties didn't seem any closer to resolving them. Understanding and tolerance, it appeared, were no more on offer now than before we had a name for my daughter's condition. A statement of educational needs was also out (for now: I wasn't giving up without a fight). So what was the great prize for which we had gone through all these tests. Was someone going to teach her social skills? To tell the time and cross the road?

Weren't her pure singing voice, her story-writing and her extraordinary drawing skills enough? And if they were enough, why did she need this label? Nobody really cared about it because it wasn't serious enough. Yet it was serious enough to call it a disability. There it was again. The D-word. To go with the A-word. Which nobody seemed to really care about. Except when they did.

As a friend of mine, Sam, put it: 'Aspergers is difficult. You don't really fit in the "normal" world and you don't really fit in the disabled world. You sort of fall through the middle.'

Sam and I go back years. She has always been a jolly

woman, ready with a smile and with a soft voice that used to make me think of marshmallows. We have kept in touch through marriages and pregnancies, sending Christmas cards and the occasional email. After months and years of brief, cheery notes post-children, we learned that behind the scenes we were both going through the same trial. I rang Sam to ask for help and advice on coping, to ask whether people understand her child any better than they do mine, and noticed that her easy tones had taken on a steely edge.

'It took me six months to say "My son has autism". When I first heard the word, I thought of mute kids banging their heads on the floor. I really worried about the label at the start,' she told me.

Sam's son Nathan, now five, was just three years old when he was diagnosed. In what I am now starting to recognise as a familiar pattern from talking to these parents, my battle-comrades, Sam's sunny toddler changed under the pressure of going to nursery school. Unlike Grace, however, he did not tune out. Instead, he started biting, lashing out, hitting. Sam told me frankly that she used to dread collecting her boy at the end of the day and hearing what he'd done. She used to think it was all her fault. She'd think: I'm a bad parent. Why can't I get my child to behave when everyone else can?

Eventually, Sam and her husband John took Nathan for a developmental check. Hearing this part of her story, I saw again how random the process is; no weeks and months and years of waiting here, but a shockingly fast diagnosis that in its very suddenness left Sam too bowled over. After half an hour, the paediatrician who was assessing Nathan told Sam and John in matter-of-fact tones that their son was definitely on the autistic spectrum, but that he would probably be OK at school.

'It was like being hit by a freight train. I went to bed and cried for the rest of the afternoon,' Sam told me.

As we chatted, I understood that there is another label that often comes with that of autism: the naughty child. Sam talked to me calmly of incidents involving other people's reactions to her son that made me boil with fury on her behalf and think how lucky Grace and I have been. My daughter's meltdowns have usually been either with me or in school, but with her teacher near by – settings where she feels safe enough to let rip. I have not suffered public displays of her violent anxiety. The inappropriate behaviour I see from Grace when we're out is relatively gentle – clutching me when a dog hoves into view, or clamping her hands over her ears when a motorbike or an ambulance passes, or striding out to cross the road without ever, ever looking (this causes me palpitations daily and, I'm sure, premature ageing). Often when we're out, Grace might dance, or pull faces, or get lost in her reflection – on whatever surface – which generally prompts smiles from other people, rather than consternation and condemnation.

Sam, however, has run the gauntlet of public hostility for years. 'It toughens you up. You become a lot harder emotionally and mentally because of the way strangers treat your children,' she explained, then gave me a list of examples that I could barely believe I was hearing: people shouting at her for using disabled toilets (because her son hates the hand-dryers in other toilets); people nudging and pointing when Nathan had a meltdown or had to be kept in a pushchair, so that he wouldn't run off; one mother – in a lift, when Nathan broke down because he couldn't push the buttons – responded to his distress with the words: 'He hasn't got a disability. He's just really naughty.'

Googling 'autistic' and 'naughty' together, it became clear to me that Sam's experience was not the exception. One of the first references thrown up by my internet search was a 2010 survey by autism charity Treehouse which found that three-quarters of parents and carers of autistic children polled believed the public thought their child was just naughty. Next, I found a piece of research finding that scores of pupils were being unfairly excluded from school because their autism was mistaken for naughty behaviour. Next up: a *Daily Mail* article which said the Work and Pensions Secretary had 'ordered a crackdown on thousands of families with youngsters diagnosed with "naughty child syndrome" who get new cars paid for by the state'. I felt no relief when it turned out that the article was, in fact, referring to Attention Deficit Hyperactivity Disorder (ADHD) – the suggestion of which appeared in brief among Grace's notes and is not a rare side order with autism diagnoses. When I came next to a site selling badges which pronounced 'I'm not Naughty, I'm Autistic', I decided to switch my computer off.

By now I had started writing about how I felt, venting my frustration and expressing my love for my poor, set-upon child in pages of notes as I travelled to and from work by train. As the stations rattled past, I would try to make sense of what was happening to us by putting it all down on paper. Then I posted some of it online and suddenly other parents were contacting me to tell me that what I had written had moved them. Many of them said to me: 'You're living my life.' Many of them have since become my friends.

'I think there's a complete lack of understanding about autism and Aspergers,' said Louise, thirty-two, mother to Ewan, who is six and also has Asperger's Syndrome. Ewan is careful and particular. Photographs of him show a lean, intent face. He likes Lego. He likes to line things up. He is phenomenally good at maths.

'When he was diagnosed, I lost count of the number of people who said to me: "Does that mean he's like Rain Man",' Louise told me in good-natured exasperation. 'They think autism means a savant, or someone who does lots of rocking and flapping, or a kid who's naughty.'

Every single parent who spoke to me on this subject used that Rain Man reference. For a film made in 1988, it still exerts a huge influence over the public's imagination and attitudes.

'Because most people with Asperger's Syndrome look "normal", people expect them to behave normally. A lot of people think of someone with autism as a person who cannot speak or, like the Dustin Hoffman character in "Rain Man",' added Amanda, forty-nine, mother to seventeen-year-old Harry, who keeps his diagnosis a secret because of his worries about how people might perceive him.

Harry was only diagnosed in his early teens: school life was going relatively smoothly because of his academic abilities, but at home his rages were becoming increasingly violent and difficult for Amanda, who is a single parent, to deal with. She told me that in some ways the diagnosis came as a relief for her – she wasn't a useless parent and Harry wasn't 'bad' – but that it opened up a host of other potential pitfalls too.

Despite knowing that Amanda's son had been violent towards her, the psychiatrist did not tell Harry his diagnosis, but left her to do so. Harry took the news very badly and refused to accept the diagnosis for more than a year, worried that his teenage peers would call him 'retarded' or something similar, and that any gossip about him would spread quickly through social networks like Facebook.

My heart goes out to Harry. I think of Grace's struggle with her own diagnosis and hope hard that she is able to hold on to her sense of being special through the difficult and sensitive years of adolescence.

It is hard, as a journalist, to hear many parents tell me that the media has contributed towards the perception of autistic children as stupid or naughty. 'The National Autistic Society does a great deal to promote awareness, but I think that the media is not always helpful,' Amanda told me, and Louise agreed.

'But it can change. The sooner we move away from sensationalism the better,' she said, speaking brightly and quickly in her Manchester accent. 'There was a programme on TV recently about children with behavioural difficulties that was called *My Child's Not Perfect*. The title really angered me. My child is perfect!'

Louise's last words pierced me. I thought of my behaviour

in the first few months after Grace was diagnosed, how I began to scrutinise her every reaction in an attempt to break it down and parse it. (Was that gesture something to do with her having Aspergers? What about that one? If not, was I sure? And if so, what was I supposed to do?) I became jumpy, frightened that I was responding wrongly to something that wasn't anything to do with her diagnosis, or that I was failing to spot and deal appropriately with other aspects of her behaviour that were. In my urgent desire to lead the way for Grace, I was starting instead to lose sight of my daughter, and in danger of allowing her to be obliterated by her label.

The one thing I clung on to was the running. That was simple. It was just putting one foot in front of the other. I couldn't mess that up. But I was starting to have to think more about precisely what message I wanted to get through to people as the awareness-raising part of my endeavour.

The National Autistic Society asked me if I was willing to participate in some local publicity for my run – the half-marathon was only a month away. I said yes, though at that point I wasn't entirely sure what I wanted to tell people who asked. 'My daughter's got this, and it's causing her some prob-lems, so can you please be a bit more understanding, while not making a big fuss' wasn't really going to do it. But it was all I had for now.

I talked to the NAS about Grace and me and signed off on a press release that was then sent to several of my local news-papers.

Friends and colleagues were still sponsoring me: amaz-ingly, the flow of generous contributions continued and I had now reached nearly nine hundred pounds. I was astonished and touched by the kindness and encouragement of people, many of whom I rarely spoke to except via Christmas cards, Facebook inanities or when we bumped into each other in the kitchen at work.

Then the first newspaper article came out and I saw what everyone else was seeing.

'Mother to run for autistic daughter' read the headline in my local press.

(Much, much later, Grace's dad told me that he'd opened his copy of the newspaper, sitting in his house, twenty minutes away down the road, and frozen. 'I felt as though you had defined her by her limitations,' he said.)

My own feelings were mixed. I was pleased at what was a fair article, giving publicity to a cause that needed it. I was pleased when some more kind souls saw the article and donated money to someone they'd never met for a cause that needed it. Grace saw it, and the photograph of us both, and smiled, and hugged me.

But that headline nagged. It made me feel uncomfortable for a reason I couldn't pin down, in the same way a well-meaning comment from a colleague at work had given me pause some weeks earlier, when he applauded my fundraising efforts and then apologised for any crass comments he might have made in the past about autistic people.

Were we both labelled now, Grace and I? Had I branded her and, in so doing, marked myself? I asked Louise the question and she told me about a work colleague who had changed his attitude towards her after finding out about

Ewan's diagnosis. 'He said, "I had no idea that Ewan had Aspergers. I'm so sorry." It made me think: does that mean that person will look at me differently from now on? I thought: why are you sorry?'

I decided to look for some positive role models for Grace. I was getting as sick of Rain Man as everyone else.

Searching the internet for famous people with Aspergers felt like an extraordinarily libellous act: countless sites exist attributing autistic or AS diagnoses to household names without, as far as I can see, any proof or confirmation from the subjects themselves.

So I went back to Amazon – again navigating that list of po-faced tomes – to seek a book for children about 'Autism Heroes'. I found one that celebrated Albert Einstein, Hans Christian Andersen and Wassily Kandinsky: the world's most famous scientist; the world's most famous storyteller; and one of the first abstract artists (and creator of singularly beautiful works).

Telling Grace that she shared attributes with all of them was a moment of pure joy. Watching her leaf through the pages and see that her brain worked the same way as the writer of *The Little Mermaid* almost moved me to tears – it was as though she had discovered a long-lost relative and the missing piece of the jigsaw and the pot of gold at the end of the rainbow, all at the same time.

We don't read that book enough. It should be in every school library.

The idea that Grace belonged to a group of 'different minds' stayed with me. For a long time, I turned over in my head thoughts of famous artists and writers and actors who had seemed to exist at a different altitude, their senses keener and their experiences both sharper or more colourful and, often, more painful. With my own recent breakdown in mind, I found myself returning frequently to the link between mental illness and unusual ways of thinking.

Then I saw an article in the *New Scientist* that asked: 'Could mental illness have been the making of our species?' It began:

In the industrialised world, roughly 1 person in every 25 has severe mental disorder and nearly half of us will experience some kind of mental illness during our lives. Many conditions, including schizophrenia and bipolar disorder, as well as developmental conditions like autism, are at least in part inherited from our parents. If they affect people's chance of survival adversely, you would expect natural selection to have eliminated them, but instead they persist at high levels.

The story moved me enormously, and cheered me. Its affirmation of different minds, and man's ability to adapt and move forward as a species by embracing them, felt like an affirmation of my daughter. I felt as though the author, Kate Ravilious, was beckoning me on to show me Grace's antecedents, to set out for me her alternative personal history and her role. The article examined the persistence of genes associated with different kinds of brain development and explored the part they might have played in enabling our race to flourish. From technological revolutions that started with spears, to bursts of artistic creativity that began with early carved figures and simple musical instruments, to unusual and creative people like shamans, the article charted the special talents in the population that have helped humans to get this far.

A particularly striking turn of phrase in the piece stayed with me: a reference to 'orchid genes' which, when nurtured, would enable their carrier to thrive, but when neglected would have the opposite effect.

I thought of Harry and his anger and his difficulty in accepting the diagnosis that would set him apart from his peers and leave him open to ridicule from some of them. How different his life would feel if instead of ostracising people with maverick minds, we could only learn to cherish them, as Ravilious suggested:

> If the special talents in the population have helped humans to get this far, we may need such different modes of thinking to see us through the next few thousand years. If the past teaches us anything, it's that humanity thrives by being adaptable.

Echoes of Grace's misery resonate in Harry's reaction to his diagnosis too: he wished that he hadn't been born. Amanda told me: 'He asked me why I hadn't had the genetic screening when I was pregnant with him and terminated the pregnancy.'

The distress of our children – their painful wondering at their existence – made me fearful for other children, and other parents who have access to that kind of screening. But when I went to find out more on the subject, I found, of course, that the experts were there way before me.

Professor Simon Baron-Cohen is director of the Autism Research Centre at the University of Cambridge. It is pretty much impossible to avoid coming across his name in any exploration of autism and related conditions. Way back in 2009, he was already warning – according to a BBC News article – that the prospect of a prenatal test for autism that would allow couples to choose whether to have a baby with the condition might also mean the loss of particular talents in the population.

I pursued Professor Baron-Cohen – via polite phone calls and emails to his charming assistant – to ask him about this directly. He is a rock star in the world of autism research and attracts crowds of followers to his theories in much the same way as his cousin, the comedian Sacha Baron-Cohen, attracts his own fans to cinema multiplexes. So I didn't hold out much hope.

But he emailed me back, and to my question – did he consider Asperger's Syndrome to be a disability – he responded: it's a mixture. The disability, he said, lies in social and communication domains, where the individual may experience high levels of social anxiety and difficulties in communication, and may find it hard to read social cues and imagine other people's points of view. He called it 'mindblindness'.

So far, so familiar. Then he said: 'But the flip side of AS are areas of ability and sometimes even talent. These tend to be in two key areas: attention to detail (where they may notice details other miss) and seeing patterns (particularly regularities that enable them to figure out "how things work"). For some people with AS it might be math, for others physics or computer science, for others it might be the natural world. For some, their fascination with a class of object may not turn into anything particularly useful for them or for society, but ... allows for the potential to do something remarkable (like run a successful niche business or make a scientific discovery or play music or create art to an extreme level).'

The label of autism and Asperger's Syndrome, he said, was useful in unlocking the help and support that people need with their difficulties. But what about the label itself, I emailed him to ask. Will there ever be a time when it stops mattering?

'I think we have seen a gradual growth in awareness of autism and AS over the decades, which is good. I hope we reach a point where such labels are accepted as easily as, for example, the label dyslexia, where there is no stigma attached to it and it is simply accepted that this person has a particular profile of strengths and difficulties,' he replied.

My heart lifted upon reading these words, and I had to edit my emailed response to him several times to get to the point where I was merely saying a grateful thank you for finding the time to respond, rather than an effusive outpouring of relief. I so much want to hope that he is right.

In the meantime, however, something extraordinary happened.

I logged on to my computer one day to find that a reader,

identifying herself as a person with Asperger's Syndrome, had written a letter to Grace on my blog. Beneath the entry in which I wrote about Grace's experiences of bullying, Debi Brown wrote what amounts to an Ode to the Joy of Aspergers. Her tenderness for Grace moved me to tears (again – it's an occupational hazard of being Grace's mother that I spend a lot of time crying, whether in distress or relief, happiness or some other form of intense emotion).

Debi's portrayal of life with AS and the loving assurances she sent to Grace about her own gifts are life-affirming. It is, in my opinion, the kindest gift any parent of a child with AS could receive. I have read it countless times and I am still incapable of reading the first and last lines without getting a lump in my throat. With Debi's generous agreement, I've reproduced her letter in full at the back of the book (see p. 254). Here is my edited version:

The Point of You:

Grace, sweetheart, listen because I think I know what the point of you is. One per cent of the population are spectrum folk. That means that you probably don't know all that many yet, but there are a lot. There are 62,300,000 people in the UK. So that means 623,000 are on the spectrum. Most of these people have not yet discovered their Aspieness. The likes of you and me don't tend to be known about at all. This causes some problems. For example, everyone tends to overreact when they get a diagnosis and imagine that things are far worse than they actually are. Also, now, when I tell people I'm an Aspie, if they know anything about the spectrum, they tend to assume that I cannot do stuff. The point is, that no one has quite understood the likes of you and me yet. The professionals get some bits right, but other bits, they can get really wrong.

It's really important that you keep believing in yourself and how incredibly capable you are. Don't let anyone tell you that you cannot do anything because of being an Aspie. It's not true. Some super-wonderful things about you are: you are very, very bright. This means that you will be able to think your way around problems that others might think would be impossible for you. You will be a great communicator. Because you are so very, very clever, you will be able to find ways around the things that are extra-difficult for you.

You are able to trust – you trust your mum enough to tell her what's happening in your life. That is so fantastic, sweetheart. This is such a good strategy for life.

You are able to love. I'm only just learning this bit now, so you are years and years ahead of me emotionally already.

You are creative – you dance, sing, act and dress up.

You're funny. This is a very attractive quality and will win you friends.

You are so, so brave. You don't give up. This is incredibly important.

You tell the truth. This is a lovely quality and people value you for this.

You give great hugs and kisses. I'm only just learning how to do this. Again, you are years ahead of me. And other people will love you for it, your whole life long.

You are not limited in your choices to what the world sees as 'normal'. This is a really valuable trait to have. It gives you a lot of wiggle-room to choose what is right for you.

I've now met a lot of Aspies. Some of them have a lot of difficulty controlling their anger. But I don't think I actually have met any Aspie who is mean. We simply aren't mean people. We are some of the nicest people on earth. There are plenty of good things about being an Aspie, and this is one of them. Lots of non-spectrum people try to manipulate others for their personal gain. Aspies don't do this. It's not in our nature. Bullies are mean because they hurt people intentionally, for no reason. That is the definition of mean. You are not mean.

Precious one, you are simply fantastic and you have a wonderful future ahead of you. You are more capable and more lovely than you can possibly know.

Lots of love,
Debi xxx

6

Autism is everywhere

Autism: *noun* a mental condition, present from early childhood, characterised by great difficulty in communicating and forming relationships with other people and in using language and abstract concepts.

Asperger's Syndrome: *noun* a rare and relatively mild autistic disorder characterised by awkwardness in social interaction, pedantry in speech and preoccupation with very narrow interests.
Oxford English Dictionary

Was it me? Was it something I did?

I have found that I watch other people's children intently. I look at the way they behave and then I look at their parents, and I wonder: what did you do that was different?

I remember the morning I found out I was pregnant with Grace.

It was a very masculine bathroom. From the yellow and black tiles, to the shabby towel slung over the back of the door, to the dog-eared copies of *NME* stacked behind the toilet. The air, still fuggy from the shower, carried traces of citrus aftershave.

From my position on the floor, I breathed it in and surveyed the small room, blinking hard. On the shelf beside the bath was a tin toy submarine, flaking in places and smudged with soap scum. Somewhere in my brain, a smile registered. It didn't make it to my face.

I leaned back against the door, willing myself to bring my right hand up in front of my face. It was like trying to command a shop dummy. I closed my eyes. When I opened them, the white stick was there, trembling in front of my face as my fingers fought to keep control. The line was still pink. Pink! *This is not happening. (Does pink mean it will be a girl?)*

I shook my head, but this time a smile, stubborn, flickered to my lips, even as the thought skittered away. Catching my reflection in the bathroom mirror, I mimed a comedy swipe to my forehead. Doh. Must have done it wrong is all. The face staring back looked sceptical. Bordering on the hysterical.

I left the bathroom and shrugged on my jacket, patting the pockets for change, then nudged back the catch on the front door and swung it shut. In the stillness of the carpeted hallway I felt as though my body vibrated with its secret message and must surely transmit it to anyone passing. She's not just popping out for milk, my heart thrummed. She's going to the chemist, my nerves sang. My hair swung and whispered – pssst, see what she did with the latch? Doesn't even have her own key. My arms felt too long, my shoes lumpy, as I wobbled down the stairs. Passing through the arch that led to the street I banged my elbow: a brief firework of pain that quickly fizzled out.

Outside it was another one of those brisk, grey April days that pass for spring in London. I turned my face up to the wind, hoping it would bring me round. I was in the chemist shop before I wanted to be, and in front of the shelves bearing rows of rectangular boxes. A ragged cardboard sign bore the fluorescent legend: two for the price of one. There were no single packets. I picked up two, huddled together under their blue cellophane, paid and hurried back along the street.

Once more in the flat, everything seemed cold and hard, and I felt out of place. Its warm morning embrace – hey, you still here? Nice to see you, have a cup of coffee from the pot he left and listen to the radio that's still on – had gone, ticking away with the radiators as the heat switched off. Normal people were at work. Or on their way there. Or busy with something else. Cleaning, tidying, taking the kids to the park . . . My handbag leaned lopsidedly against the sofa where I had placed it in readiness for the morning, notebook spilling out over expensive leather shoes lined up beside it. A still life, neatly encapsulating my job, which I loved; my recent promotion, which still delighted me; my salary, which though hardly investment-banker grade was enough for a single person to have fun with. Already it seemed like someone else's life. I took a deep breath, puffed out my cheeks and headed back into the bathroom. Fifteen minutes later I was still in there, but comparing three pink lines. *So that's that then*. And I burst out laughing.

Still laughing, I grabbed my belongings and left, half-running towards the main road while simultaneously trying to punch numbers into my mobile phone. I sprinted through the underpass, hopping for a moment while pulling on a shoe properly, and screwed my eyes shut as I waited for the ringing to connect with a familiar male voice. At some point during the breathless, half-garbled message I blurted into the answering machine, I realised I was crying.

The following weeks were slow and sticky as treacle. Grace's dad kept nodding and looking at a spot somewhere on the horizon and saying: 'It's OK. It's OK. It's OK.' I trawled bookshops for handbooks and then was too afraid to open them once I got them home. Sitting at the window of my tiny, pretty flat, I would look at the cherry blossom in the trees and the row of shops opposite. Trendy women with wonky fringes flitted in and out of brightly promising second-hand clothes shops. Men in camouflage trousers and beanie hats slouched in wicker chairs outside the Lebanese café. London life. I would gaze down at it from my room – my lovely, stylish, clutter-free room – and lace my fingers together to suppress the urge to hold a cigarette and think: *not now. Not now. I've got things to do.* But somehow, my mind would not let in an alternative. At the first signal that there was another option it shut down, turned black, filled the screen with snow. Instead, it preferred to turn over the idea of a baby. Peered at it and prodded it and went away to sulk and storm and sob. But it kept checking over its shoulder to see it was still there.

Work went on and I turned up. The buses and the Tube kept running. Newspapers were produced, every day. Television programming didn't falter. I held my thirtieth birthday party in a trendy bar, pretended there was rum in my Coke and punctuated the evening with surreptitious trips to the toilet where I nibbled on ginger biscuits and took long, even breaths. Friends regarded me with narrowed glances.

A month later, Grace's dad and I had a belting row in an Indian restaurant on Westbourne Grove, fiery with hot food that gave me miserable indigestion and him a raging thirst. In the weeks since my discovery, I had been blindsided by a craving for sleep and peace that had not sat well with his for alcohol and cigarettes and company. We sat trading resentful barbs. Hoping to shock him into realising our new circumstances, I smoked cigarettes and drank wine, daring him to criticise, hoping he would quail. Ferocious and lost, we glared at each other. Around us, the talk was of parties, clubs, movies and events. I inhaled the acrid smoke and, as the nicotine cudgelled its way through my bloodstream, wondered, again, what on earth I was doing. What on earth I was.

The answer came to me the following morning. I lay alone in my bed, head hammering. Awake since dawn and cold with fear, I had tried to make myself sick and had then drunk gallons of water which only made me feel even more bilious. Swallowing a vitamin pill, I imagined it sloshing lonely on tsunami-like waves, engaged in a futile battle with the hordes of toxins currently ransacking my body. Worse still, I imagined a little bean cowering in my womb, wondering what was going on, choked and nauseous. I put my hands across my tender stomach and said out loud: 'I'm so sorry. Please stay with me. I have no idea how this will work out. But it will be OK.'

Several weeks later, I had my first scan. I confided to the Australian nurse my fears about what my reckless night might have done. The nurse scowled and tutted as she rolled back the waistband of my trousers, pushed up my T-shirt and applied jelly to my stomach. I lay back against the crackling paper lining the hospital bed. Grace's dad cleaned his glasses on his shirt to mask the trembling of his hands. Moments later we were staring at the fragile, froggy tracing of our daughter's fingers as she put them to her mouth. The outline of her nose was his.

Later I was encouraged to undergo tests for which I qualified – at thirty – as an 'older' mum. I wonder now whether my age contributed to Grace's diagnosis. I wonder whether her dad's age – three years older than me – was significant. I wonder whether something that happened to me at some other point in my life laid the basis for the kind of child my firstborn would be. And, as I become more and more aware of the statistics, I realise that there are armies of parents wondering the same thing.

According to the National Autistic Society, around 1 in 100 people in the UK has autism. Recent statistics from America's Centre for Disease Control suggest the trend is accelerating in that country: data stating that 1 in 88 children and 1 in 54 boys has autism sparked a national outcry and debate about what might be causing the increase. Over the past twenty years there has been a sevenfold jump in autism rates in developed countries. As I read, and researched, I discovered that Grace and I were part of a trend. It felt both less lonely and more frightening at the same time.

So I started looking for someone who might know some of the answers. I found Peter Bearman, an American sociologist. Professor of Social Sciences at Colombia University, he has spent the past five years unpicking the boom in diagnoses of autism and looking at the causes behind it. His research is referred to in almost every article on the subject and his photograph – that of a lean bespectacled man in his fifties with rumpled salt-and-pepper hair – pops up regularly. He appears in many, many video clips on YouTube on the subject; I watched him in conversation several times, every fourth word going over my head, then decided to phone him to ask if he could explain it for me.

It was 9.30 a.m. New York time when I called Peter and he sounded bright, cheerful and friendly. In London it was grey and miserable and I was hunched over my notepad ready to take notes at high speed, hoping that baby Betty would not wake up from her nap and that the school would not phone to say Grace was having another bad day and could I come and get her.

So I got to the point fast.

'Why is autism suddenly everywhere?' I asked.

Peter sounded momentarily taken aback. 'Well, that's the million-dollar question and I don't know the answer.'

Ah, I thought. This isn't going the way I thought it would. I was, at least, getting used to there never being any straight-forward answers.

However, Peter was being modest. He's got a good part of the answer. He also has data on 8 million children in California, which shows that in a specific area of that state autism diagnoses in children jumped 600 per cent between 1992 and 2002.

'I think that our work has accounted for about half of that increase,' he told me, and proceeded to break it down.

Around a quarter of the increase, he explained, can be accounted for by changes in the way autism is diagnosed: previously a child with autism would have been diagnosed with 'mental retardation'. The phrase is electric, and for a moment I feel the air shimmer around me. For this to have been Grace's diagnosis given her abilities makes me feel sick. Peter goes on: the fact that doctors are now trained to see autism – at both ends of the spectrum, both severe and high-functioning cases, such as Aspergers – means that they can accurately diagnose cases.

I may have felt ill at the thought of 'mental retardation' being the explanation given to me, but Peter explains that for a long time, a diagnosis of autism had the same effect on parents. A further quarter of the recent increase in autism rates, he told me, comes from the fact that doctors and parents are now accepting the diagnosis as an option. This is a huge about-turn from the 1960s and '70s, when autism was heavily stigmatised. The thinking was that children who had autism were psychologically damaged by their parents.

'There was a lot of stigma for parents to have children with autism. They faced a diagnosis with trepidation. When it became clear that it was a developmental disorder, it freed up doctors and made it possible for them to more accurately diagnose children,' Peter told me.

Behind his concise summary lies a scandal, which I discovered with horror when I did some more research after our talk. From the 1950s until relatively recently, mothers of children with autism were told it was their fault. Termed 'refrigerator mothers' for what psychologists said was their coldness and inability to love their children, generations of women were betrayed and branded psychotic by a medical community in thrall to Bruno Bettelheim, an Austrian-born American child psychologist.

Born in 1903, Bettelheim was Jewish by birth and, as a young man, was incarcerated in the concentration camps of Dachau and Buchenwald. He based much of his theory about autistic children on his experience there and popularised the 'refrigerator mother' theory that was first proposed by another American psychiatrist, Leo Kanner, who in 1949 highlighted what he found to be 'a genuine lack of maternal warmth' in mothers of autistic children.

In the most extreme expression of Bettelheim's thinking, this concept suggested that mothers simply did not want their children to exist, that they wanted their children dead in the same way that the Nazis wanted all Jews to be dead.

While this avenue of exploration was almost unbearable, I decided to continue along it for a time and discovered an excellent, award-winning documentary made in 2003 – *Refrigerator Mothers*, directed by David Simpson – which talked to women now in their fifties and sixties about the trauma of seeking help for their children, only to have been separated from them and subjected to years of psychoanalysis themselves.

'It wasn't so much the child that was the patient as it was the parents,' one mother, June Francis, says in the film: 'I thought: what have we done that is so awful that would drive a child into such a regression? I was told I had not connected or bonded with the child because of inability to properly relate to the child and that this was autism. I couldn't quite see how that could happen. But here was someone of authority telling me that it had happened ...

'It was so horrifying to think of this darling little child that you're going to separate yourself from. But they said: if you love your child, you will do this.'

Lorraine Roberts told the camera that her psychologist had 'tried to make me believe that my father was disappointed in me. I tried to believe that he was a bad father and that my mother didn't love me. But I looked back and I thought: it was a pretty happy childhood.'

I watched this film choked and appalled, fervently thankful that research has moved on. The discovery that autism was a neurological disorder to which one could not apply Freudian methods halted Bettelheim's ascendancy, and his research funding. Children were returned to their parents, their mothers told that all was now well.

The guilt I feel about whether I missed something, or could do more for Grace, pales in comparison to what these women have suffered.

'I have fought this battle with bitterness within my soul because I didn't find out for years that I wasn't at fault, for sure. And I can't quite overcome it. I'm trying. But there's no answer to this place inside my soul,' says Lorraine Roberts at the end of the film. 'I can't get down there and dig it out. I just can't. It's simply a result of the analysis.'

Watching the documentary, I was struck by the youth of the mothers. As they narrated their early lives, montages of black and white photographs showed smiling post-war brides, unaware of the anguish that lay just around the corner. Many were not even twenty when they had their children.

All of them were younger than me.

Back to Peter, who confirmed: 'Ten per cent of the increase in autism diagnoses we have seen is to do with relatively major demographic change, which is that parents are older.'

Basically, he said, it has been established that as women get older and have more children at an older age, those children are at greater risk of developmental disorder. In addition, women are marrying older men, who also contribute to that risk. And because women are having their children later they are having them closer together – and these closely spaced pregnancies bring added risk.

I held my breath when Peter told me he was now also conducting research – not yet concluded or published when we spoke – about the possible impact of assisted reproductive technologies (IVF) on autism diagnoses. He believed that there may be something that causes both autism and infertility, or that something in the IVF process, such as the hormones given to women to prepare them for the treatment, could pose, as he put it, 'a neurodevelopmental risk'.

'In California now, 2 per cent of all births are in-vitro births. I think there's an additional risk from that, but we won't know the answer until later in the year,' he told me. 'It's not a smoking gun, but it's an important piece of the puzzle.'

Another big factor in the boom is cultural awareness of autism. Parents think about their children's development and autism is now part of their vocabulary. We can help doctors diagnose autism in children where twenty years ago they didn't have the skills at their disposal.

But many of the parents who take their child to the family doctor with worries about a possible autism diagnosis do so because they believe some other factor has caused it. Among the mothers and fathers I talked to, nearly every one had pinpointed some other factor and asked themselves : 'Was it *that*?'

'I wonder if it's anything to do with me working as a dental nurse before I had Sophie. I was around chemicals and mercury between the ages of sixteen and thirty,' said Nic. 'Or if it's to do with her stressful birth. I had a C-section and for a baby they're not ready, are they? Suddenly they're yanked out into the world.'

It would take me another book to list the many suspected causes of autism, so I've summarised just a very few of them here. The big one, of course, and the one that very many parents still find hard to ignore, is the MMR vaccine, which protects children against measles, mumps and rubella. I had Grace inoculated and noticed no difference in her at the time. I admit though to a flicker of wonder after her diagnosis, even though to me, at least, the claim that MMR causes autism has been roundly disproved. The claim was brought by British doctor Andrew Wakefield, who was subsequently found guilty of serious professional misconduct for the way in which he had carried out his research. But for some, the argument that multiple vaccines can overload a child's system remains too powerful to discount.

As the number of diagnoses mushrooms, so too do the suggested reasons for it and, more lately, elements of modern life like television and electricity power lines have been subjected to scrutiny for their effect on young minds.

As far as Peter was concerned, environmental factors in today's world can be discounted. For starters, he said, the environment we live in today is healthier than the one we grew up in when DDT was being sprayed around. (As he tells me this, a line from a favourite Joni Mitchell song of my mother's floats through my mind, and I remember the worried attention she gave to newspapers and television news reports on the subject of pesticides when I was a child.)

'The environment is better than it was thirty or forty years ago. And if you look for autism within an environment of incredible environmental degradation, you don't see it. So I don't think there's something in the pollution of our environment that's doing it,' Peter said. 'The California data, which shows a cluster of cases of autism, disproves the case for some of the other suggested environmental causes of autism, like television or vaccines or high electricity wires. Those other things are found everywhere, so they cannot be the cause for the incidence of autism that were found only in one place.'

However, he continued: 'It's possible that the environment you grew up in could have had an impact on the children that you have. It's not about now, but about what it was like when your mother was carrying you. It would explain a local cluster of the kind we've found that could be down to an environmental contaminant from generations ago that's gone now.

'If I'm right, you should see a decline of autism in the next years.'

That evening, I went for a run, diving out of the door almost as soon as my husband came in from work, desperate for air and thinking time. I took a long, flat cycle route and let my legs do their work while my mind returned to what Peter had said. The idea of a temporary swelling of autism cases, followed by a retreat in numbers nagged at me. Will this mean that Grace's generation will be peculiarly unique? I wondered. Was she destined to spend her life with this sense of isolation?

I didn't want to go home again that evening. I wanted to run and run until my sense of unease had lifted. I paced until dusk had turned to night and returned home to a worried husband, whose face crumpled with relief when I finally walked back in through the door.

Shortly afterwards, I found research to counter my concern – from Simon Baron-Cohen again – whose findings suggested that people with a lot of autistic traits are now meeting and marrying and having autistic children together.

He pointed out that in the last twenty years, more and more women have moved into the fields of technology, engineering and science – areas to which men with a lot of autistic traits are typically attracted because of their tendency towards what Baron-Cohen calls 'systemising'. That is, that ability to see patterns and figure out how things work to which he'd referred in his emails to me.

Additionally the dotcom boom at the beginning of the twenty-first century created new communities with concentrations of technologically gifted people, more 'systemisers' who were working for the growing IT industry and forming relationships with each other.

In June 2011 Baron-Cohen published the results of a survey of more than 62,000 schoolchildren in the Netherlands which showed that two to four times as many children in Eindhoven – the capital of Dutch industrial design and technology, sometimes referred to as the Dutch Silicon Valley – had been diagnosed with autism as children in Haarlem and Utrecht, which have similar socioeconomic profiles, but far fewer technology industry workers.

By this reckoning, I thought, and given the constant and growing importance of scientific advance, computer science and technology in our lives, it would seem that the communities who research and invent and provide – and attract and give birth to other people diagnosed with a lot of autistic traits – can only grow too.

Unless, of course, someone hits upon a cure.

As things stand, the main 'treatment' comes in the form of support, and for high-functioning autism like Grace's, that primarily means learning. There is a raft of educational techniques and assistance available. Though God knows in my part of the world it seems extraordinarily hard to access (more of this later), this was the route I had started down with Grace. I had seen examples of people with high-functioning autism who were able to adapt and learn how to socialise and overcome their communication difficulties, while retaining their individuality and often, indeed, being prized for their particular (and many) skills. ·

But for many parents, among them – naturally enough – those whose children suffer from severe autism, this is not sufficient. Some who are desperate for more radical help to change and improve the lives of their children want alternative therapies.

Researching the options on offer in this universe felt like stepping into Aladdin's cave: before me lay acres of winking treasures – endless bounty that somehow also seemed liable to leave me empty-handed if I grasped for them. Thousands upon thousands of case studies are out there, detailing the differences that can be made by everything from drugs, to diet (cutting out gluten, dairy products, caffeine and sugar being the most common), to dolphin therapy and dogs for autism. Intensive behavioural training exists in many different forms and programmes; music, light and sound therapy is also popular. I even discovered the 'Audiokinetron' – an electronic machine to exercise the entire hearing system, with the aim of improving sound sensitivity and thus reducing behavioural disturbances.

In every instance, a proponent would rave about the changes effected. Someone else would declare it bunkum.

I asked Peter Bearman if the work he was doing would

result, ultimately, in a cure. Do you, I asked, foresee a treatment?

This time his answer was unequivocal.

'Yes. According to our data, about 10 per cent of children with autism who start off severely impacted have incredible developmental trajectories and are off the spectrum within a decade. Something is happening to those children,' he said.

'And as soon as you can see that some kids really do change in different ways, you have to ask what are their parents doing?'

Bearman can't do the study himself: as part of the research conditions for his other work the names and personal details of the families and children he has studied have been erased. He is following 8 million children, but he doesn't know who they are, or what their parents did, or what services they used. But if someone else does a study and finds those children and observes what they're doing, he says, 'I'm sure that what's accessible to 10 per cent of all children can be of use to many more.'

It's tantalising to think that the seed of knowledge about how to cure this condition may already be out there in the population somewhere.

But when I think about a 'cured' version of Grace, my mind draws a blank. I find I don't know who that is. Where does my daughter begin and her Aspergers end? How can she be Grace without being all that she is now?

The whole idea of somehow 'fixing' autism is of course a highly controversial area and there is a growing movement among adults with autism and Asperger's Syndrome to oppose any attempts to 'cure' the disorder. They emphasise instead the importance of celebrating difference.

Aspies for Freedom is one such group. An online forum founded by a group of people with Asperger's Syndrome in June 2004, it aims to bring together people with autism-spectrum conditions to further the view that Aspergers and autism are not negative, and not always a disability.

'Part of the problem with the "autism as tragedy" point of view is that it carries with it the idea that a person is somehow separable from autism, and that there is a "normal" person trapped "behind" the autism,' says the homepage on the group's website. It continues:

> Being autistic is something that influences every single element of who a person is – from the interests we have, the ethical systems we use, the way we view the world and the way we live our lives. As such, autism is part of who we are ...
>
> We know that autism is not a disease and we oppose any attempts to 'cure' someone of an autism-spectrum condition, or any attempts to make them 'normal' against their will.

I read this and stop dead. Is this what I have been doing? Have I been trying to make my darling girl 'normal'?

There are many similar groups and thousands of proponents. There are also thousands of parents and the deeper I go into the argument on cyberspace, the louder the shouting gets. Just as I thought I was starting to get a grip on the scale of the community to which my daughter – and therefore to a certain extent I too – now belongs, the rug is pulled out from under me again. Now I have to answer the question of just how committed we are to being part of this community or whether we've been trying to be something else.

I think back to the very many testimonies on treatments I read and I wonder at how hard it must be for parents of severely autistic children to support any idea that says attempts to cure are iniquitous and insulting.

And then, just like that, I find an answer for me and for Grace.

It's a Sunday afternoon and the ham I am boiling in the kitchen has caused the windows to steam up, giving the outside world an opaque, distant appearance. Betty is asleep and Grace is at her dad's house and I am for the time being alone, sitting at the dinner table surfing websites and turning the pages of a growing pile of books beside my computer. My head is spinning. I have tried several times to get up and walk away and allow my jumbled, gyrating thoughts to come to a stop – to let them fall where they will and leave me to pick over the pieces later. But I can't quite do it.

And then I click on a site called Neurodiversity.com, whose stated aims are to reduce the challenges of autism and help increase education and support. On the page dealing with the question of a cure is an excerpt from a quote which makes my heart beat a bit faster. I sit up and quickly, quickly, fire up the search engine to find the rest of it.

The quote is from e.e. cummings and it feels like oxygen. It's all the answer I need, for now.

To be nobody-but-yourself – in a world which is doing its best, night and day, to make you everybody else – means to

fight the hardest battle which any human being can fight;
and never stop fighting.

I determine to let Grace be herself: to cherish and delight in
her and work hard to help others to understand and appreciate her. I can help her by getting her the support she needs
to be happy within herself, and to take pleasure in her idiosyncrasies, without worrying about where they come from or
what that means.

At least, I'll try ...

7

Do put your daughter on the stage

I am sitting on a tiny orange chair. It has a tiny bucket seat and four tiny black legs. This chair would be tiny for an Oompa Loompa. I am not an Oompa Loompa and I am exceptionally uncomfortable. I have twisted my legs up and around and hunched my back to try to fit my six-foot frame into this tiny space.

Beside me a newly fitted air-conditioning unit blows Siberian gusts into my ear.

I cannot move or complain. The curtain is about to go up.

The pianist begins – a few jolly notes – and two young girls step forward and begin to sing earnestly to each other, only the faintest tremble indicating their nervousness. The tremble is amplified and broadcast around the big room, where rows of adults sit, tense and obedient as leg muscles start to cramp.

Guitars and drums now join the song, swelling the melody

and only just failing to drown out the sounds made by excited ranks of small people being assembled backstage. The curtain bulges alarmingly, then suddenly eases, disgorging a pod of children who take their place at the side of the stage.

And there is Grace, right at the front, singing like every line is a hallelujah, her face lit up with happiness. Her kohl-rimmed eyes are huge and as she turns to address the main players my breath catches at the beauty of her profile.

As she turns back to face the audience she sees me and without faltering flashes me a brilliant smile. Her make-up shimmers and sparks. She is the most joyful I have seen her for months.

Later, Grace sings four lines alone, proud and sweet. She has practised them for days. It is her big moment but the microphone has not been switched on and no one can hear her. At the back of the room, the music teacher flaps her arms in panic and the assembled parents, with the timing of old pros, obligingly join in the chorus. Grace is oblivious, her joy undimmed.

Later that evening, I line up children in our bathroom and set about removing stage paint. J, my elder stepson, is a cheeky tiger in elaborate orange, yellow and black stripes. D, my younger stepson, is a mutely mortified wildebeest, daubed entirely brown, so that the whites of his discomfited eyes gleam in stark relief. It takes several baby wipes and a douse under the tap, but, eventually, I reclaim their sweet little boy faces.

With Grace I wipe and wipe and wipe. Carefully, over and over.

But nothing removes her sparkle.

Her great-grandmother would have been so proud – Anne Fielding (stage name Anne Malone): singer, actress and model. Clouds of blonde bouffant hair and perfume, and a laugh that would make passing strangers look up and smile. Every time Grace is assessed anew, the expert asks: 'Are there any eccentrics in the family?' and I think of Nana and her expansive gestures and the way she lived her life, as though we'd paid for her to put on a good show.

Like the time she came to visit us in our new house.

When I was fourteen, my parents moved from Glasgow, where we had lived through perpetually inclement weather and 1970s grot – rain, drunks, rain, dog shit, rain and pitched battles between football supporters amid the town-centre shops of Sauchiehall Street. In the mid-1980s the place was transformed into a cleaned-up City of Culture with a huge new museum, sandblasted warehouses of golden stone and countless Italian delicatessens (though, sadly, no amount of funding could halt the precipitation).

At this point, as Europe looked interestedly into its latest investment, we moved out, to a tiny university village in the middle of England. Keele is sandwiched between Manchester and Birmingham and known to many primarily for its service station on the M6. My father had been made a professor of French and head of department at the age of thirty-eight (now two years older than he was then, I can appreciate why we galloped south to grab this opportunity) and we took up residence in one of the campus houses designated for professors. It was a detached, square 1950s' red-brick with a swing roped around a fetchingly lopsided apple tree in the front garden, and a rowan tree in the back garden that tapped on my bedroom window whenever the wind blew. There was a red Bakelite telephone on top of the piano, parquet hallways and a cream Aga in the kitchen.

I hated it. I wanted our top-floor flat with high corniced ceilings, stripped wooden floorboards, leaning piles of books, pot plants, green brocade curtains and hippy charm – not to mention the William Morris tiles in the entrance hall.

That's a lie. All those things I remember now and appreciate. At the time, all I could think was that I was leaving my friends behind in what was now a trendy metropolis, bursting with cool nightlife, for a quiet countryside commune. My parents, who had had bohemian friends, held boisterous all-night parties and let me pedal my bike around the house for hours on Sundays until their hangovers abated, had suddenly morphed into respectable academic types.

(I hadn't yet realised there was a Student Union ten minutes' walk from my new front door. But that's another story.)

Anyway, here's the point: this was when Nana came to stay.

Nana didn't come to stay very often because she was so busy. We had our other Nana for Christmases, Easter holidays and birthdays – my mum's mum Freda, who would shower us with kisses and hugs and presents several times a year, arriving from Sunderland with exclamations of 'Eeeeee!' upon seeing how much bigger and older we had got since her last visit.

Celebrity Nana, my dad's mum, would send us birthday cards with her latest newspaper clipping in them. Or signed photographs of the cast of *Coronation Street* – which we didn't watch, TV being strictly regulated in our house – where she appeared regularly among the soap opera's stars as an extra in the Rovers Return pub.

In 1941, at the age of twenty-one, Anne had won a BBC talent competition and went on from there to earn a living by singing in clubs across the north of England. (Years later, she would show us her publicity pictures from this time and my sister and I would gawp at the glamour of the black and white photographs from which she gazed soulfully – mascara'd and festooned in paste jewellery – beyond the lens.)

Then she met my grandfather, an erect, sandy-haired man called Douglas who had fought fascists in Italy during the Second World War and came home to be a policeman. She had two children with him – my dad and his sister Susan – and was pregnant with a third child Dianne when Douglas died suddenly and unexpectedly following a minor operation. My dad was seven years old. Anne was thirty-four.

She picked up her singing career again, and branched out into acting and modelling. By day, she ran a boarding house in Knott End, situated on the southern side of Morecambe Bay, a ferry journey from Fleetwood and a short bus ride from Blackpool. By night, she transfigured herself into a gleaming alter ego who could captivate the room with her breathless singing and who caused my dad – bowed over his homework at the back – huge mortification with her audience interaction: a wink here, a shimmy there, a tousle of the hair for the man in the front row.

By the time she came to visit us in Keele, Anne was giving

piano and singing lessons to local drama students, as well as modelling knitwear for the likes of *Woman* magazine and still continuing to take the train to Manchester for her regular sessions at Granada television studios. She was in her late sixties and was never seen without perfect Marilyn Monroe waves and a touch of Clinique lipstick. Arriving at our new front door, the first thing she said on seeing my all-black ensemble – armed with a set of crimpers, I had commenced my teenage Goth phase – was: 'Khaki and rose are the colours this season, my love. Khaki, and a nice bit of rose.' Then she waved at me and went off to find the piano.

I can't remember what time of year it was but I think perhaps it must have been spring or maybe summer – because I do recall that when she opened the French windows in our sitting room, it didn't feel cold. My mum was so proud of that sitting room. (Always the sitting room, never the lounge.) We had an open fire, a chaise-longue, a pretty chest of drawers and those lovely latticed windows which led on to a wide green garden and a patio on which to drink gin and tonic. It was a room for discussing Gide, Malraux and the other French writers studied in such detail by my father the intellectual. It was a room in which my mother the linguist would curl up and read A. S. Byatt or Margaret Drabble when she had finished marking her students' Russian language essays or German comprehensions. In the kindling basket by the fire were crumpled bundles of the *Guardian* newspaper. Dotted about were occasional tables for trays of tea in china cups. My dad's chair was the one with the standard lamp beside it, so that when he came in to join us from his study he could see properly to continue his annotations among the small print of his French manuscripts.

The piano, an upright model in burnished beech, stood in the corner of the room. Nana sat down in front of it and perused the sheet music I was currently trying to master. I believe there may have been some Bach and possibly a spot of Mozart in my portfolio at the time as I was practising (somewhat listlessly) for my Grade 5 exams. Nana kept flicking until she found an old book of show tunes, and plumped for 'Edelweiss', the sentimental ode to Austria's white flower, sung with such anti-Nazi fervour in Rogers and Hammerstein's classic *The Sound of Music*.

Then, with the French windows wide open, she played the tune and sang along in full throat, emoting every word in a shimmering vibrato that would have been heard by everyone within a 3-mile radius. Nana never used the soft pedal, but would work the loud pedal like a Tour de France champion, while adding a gaudy frill to the notes of every left-hand accompaniment.

In precisely two and a half minutes, my parents' genteel cover had been blown.

Therein lay the dynamics of our relationship with her: pride warring with embarrassment. Nana loved to perform. She didn't socialise well and got bored easily. She wasn't particularly interested in hearing about other people and she couldn't settle to read a book. But she told a good story like no other, even if they were usually about herself, and when given centre stage she was the best company you could ask for.

My dad – cerebral philosopher and would-be ascetic (if only the women he lived with would stop turning up the thermostat) – spoke of her with love and exasperation and was frequently reduced to disconcerted silence in her presence. I will never forget the look on his face when she announced over dinner that she planned to apply for them both to participate together in TV's *The Generation Game.*

Blessedly, her television choices improved and in the latter years of her career Nana became unexpectedly hip. In delighted relief, we could now tell our friends about her spot in the audience for *The Mrs Merton Show* (skimming over her several appearances meantime in *Emmerdale* as Granny Dingle). Nana discovered a whole new level of celebrity as one of comedienne Caroline Aherne's 'girls'. (For those who do not know, *Mrs Merton* was a spoof interview show which featured a young comedienne dressed up as a grandmother who would ask naively blunt questions of a range of celebrities while being cheered on by an audience of real OAPs. It was never entirely clear whether her audience was in on the act.) Nana was among the group that was flown to Las Vegas for a special edition of the programme. There, she made her mark by singing 'Please Release Me' to the studio guest Engelbert Humperdinck, who had originally topped the charts with it.

Nana died on 6 October 2000, the same day I kissed Grace's father for the first time. I so wish she and Grace could have met. I so wish they could have sung together. I so wish I could have had the chance to watch them fight over who got to tell the punchline.

I watch Grace and I see her dramatic talents and I think of Nana and know that this is what she will do with her life. I am glad that she has this.

But I worry for her still: it will not be an easy career and the skill and dedication of those who are talented entertainers requires still more skill and dedication and dogged patience these days, as they battle the toxic by-product of the *X Factor* machine. The scramble for celebrity, based on no more than a desire to be famous for its own sake, has, I think, tainted the dramatic arts as a career, and Grace will have to work hard to show what she's made of. But she is nothing if not single-minded.

I worry too that working as an actor or a singer will widen even further the gulf between Grace and real life and I worry that she lacks the social skills and street smarts to navigate such a cut-throat industry. I worry about her ability to follow a plot and tune in to what is going on beyond her own performance.

So as I pursue her teachers and health workers to plot the right academic course for her and provide the educational support she needs, I am also inducting her in an appreciation of film and drama, with an eye to her subsequent training. I take her to ballet, musicals and films. I show her the fun and the skill and the hard work of it all: the beauty of Cinderella's pretty pirouettes and the heart-hammering adrenaline rush of the massive West End numbers. We talk about how she can do this too and she sings and dances all the way home.

At nine years old, Grace doesn't have the luxury of think-ing she can do anything she wants. The world is not her oyster. She is baffled by too much of it, and bored by much of the rest. She may not be able to sit eight or nine or ten GSCEs and look at the results and think about whether she would prefer a career in law, or teaching, or medicine. But she does have this rare talent to entertain, and I am determined to help her make her way along this path.

But still, there is that gulf.

By now we are in August, deep summer. I rise early every day to dress in formal attire and climb aboard the train to go to a glass office, where I sit at a desk and work, but my head and heart tell me it is holiday time, and my thoughts are those of a nine-year-old.

Summer holidays are light nights; sitting in the garden until late, inhaling the smell of grass and petrol fumes as the sky turns peach at twilight; a quart of sweets in a crumpled paper bag while devouring a pile of library books; counting out spending money from Nana; and a family outing to see the big summer film.

I am a child of the eighties, so the films we saw were big, colourful blockbusters with special effects that we discussed later in awestruck tones. They were punctuated by music that dominated the radio channels for weeks and featured soft-faced boy actors on whom to practise early crushes. *E.T.*, *Star Trek*, *Gremlins* – these were summer to me. *Ghostbusters*, and that electro-pop theme tune. *Superman*, after which my mum whooshed up and down the hall with a red towel tucked in the neck of her jumper to make me and my sister giggle.

So I took Grace to see *Super 8*, a film about kids in

summertime, billed as a cross between *E.T.* and *The Goonies*, made by a skilled new director and blessed by King Spielberg. My mum came too, minus the red towel. We bought pick 'n' mix sweeties – ribbons of fluorescent plastic and sour sugar-encrusted orbs that seemed unchanged since 1981. We sat back into seats that were fake leather. We watched with excited anticipation as the adverts and the trailers rolled past and the film began.

The opening scene featured grave-faced adults in black suits standing in a kitchen, murmuring in concerned tones about how the father would cope. In the next room, a group of kids wearing dental braces and shaggy hairdos made bad-taste jokes about the state of the buffet and the state of the body. Outside, a boy dressed in an uncomfortable-looking suit sat lonely on a swing in the snow, tracing the outline of a woman's pendant with his fingers.

At this point, Grace leaned over and asked at a normal volume: 'Why is he sad?'

I shushed her gently and explained.

A couple of minutes later she asked another question and again I reminded her to whisper, and explained what was happening.

Not long afterwards, the special effects kicked in, with eye-watering pyrotechnics and crashes and bangs that rolled around the room from multiple speakers. Grace put her fingers in her ears, where they remained for the rest of the film. From then on, I watched the film in between watching her observing what was playing out in front of her. From time to time, she would ask me why I was laughing and then file away my answer. Regularly, she asked me, 'Why did he do that?' and, 'What is happening?' Each time I told her and she said, 'Oh', and put her fingers back into her ears.

I so wanted to share this experience with her. It felt like we were communicating through glass.

At the end of the film, the music swelled, the characters embraced, the special effects provided a final shiver of excitement and the audience exhaled as one. It was stirring stuff – the moment to laugh and ruffle your kid's hair, or lean in for a kiss and surreptitiously blink away a tear. I found I was very close to crying.

On the way home, I asked Grace what her favourite part of the film was. 'The end,' she answered simply. 'I liked what they did when the words went up.'

Now, this doesn't quite signal the detachment you might think. The credits were a movie within a movie, the kind of detailed, different perception of a bigger event that Grace loves and to which she pays rapt attention. But as I drove us back, I worried again about her ability to follow the story, to see events around her, to keep up with what everyone else is seeing.

I worry about this a lot, and I do a lot of that worrying in the car, as we chat on the way to and from school or outings. Grace is starting to anticipate and deflect my poorly disguised enquiries into her activities, continually asking for music so that she doesn't have to 'do' a conversation.

Grace loves music, and can nail a tune and lyrics within minutes of hearing them (if she's interested). I fight in vain to be allowed to listen to Radio 4, but as the ensuing groaning protest – 'Noooooo! Not the NEWS!' – means I cannot hear a word, I give in and we switch instead to a series of music stations, channel-hopping whenever the adverts come on. As we jump across the airwaves, we find ourselves following a song which is being newly promoted by several stations. Grace hears it twice and when it pops up a third time, she sings along. Her voice soars and resonates around the car. She is word- and pitch-perfect and her glorious rendition puts to shame that of the weedy boy singer on the radio.

Grace has gone to various drama clubs since she was very small, as I sought an outlet for her eccentricities. At first I thought that if she got it all out of her system on Saturdays she might have space come Monday morning for the more mundane process of learning. Of course, this proved not to be the case, but her drama teachers would perk up and smile and wave when she arrived. They would raise their eyebrows at me and nod smilingly. I picked up the signals and paid the next set of fees.

Grace now goes to a three-hour class on Saturday mornings, where she learns singing, acting and dance. This means another set of end-of-term shows for her dad and I to attend. At the last one we walked in with a good idea of what to expect and, to begin with, that is what we saw. The show this time was a revue, a collection of song and dance and dramatic excerpts done by small groups of children aged five to sixteen. There was some clumsy declaiming from stolid teenagers, who moved their whole bodies shoulders first, plank-like, while reciting their lines across the echoing space of the stage to one another. Then there was some spirited dancing from two street-smart boys who wriggled, body-popped and bounced, to cheers from the audience. Then there was a boy quietly singing alone, so nervous that he had to break off several times to gulp. And then there was a big musical number involving a shuffling, stamping horde who mumbled all the words as they concentrated on their foot-work, entirely eclipsed by a gorgeous, tiny sprite at the front with a bouncing mop of dark curls and no front teeth.

Then Grace walked on to the stage alone, dressed simply in black T-shirt and black leggings. She sat on the stage with her legs swinging and waited for her cue. The music began and she started to sing. She had no microphone. But her voice was pure and sweet and clear, with a lilt that could break your heart, and she had learned to project every word up and over us and right to the back of the hall with seemingly no effort. It was like being showered in gold confetti. At the end, every-one clapped and whooped. Her teacher, standing by the front, executed a little mock bow, grinning at Grace as my daugh-ter exited the stage. I caught a mum in one of the rows in front of me turn and pull a face at her neighbour. I recognised that face. It was the same as the girls' in the playground: the face of jealousy and of knowing that this is something dif-ferent. I wanted to slap her. Instead I clapped harder.

When I think of Nana now, I think of my dad's face at her funeral. I think of him visibly shaking with the effort of not breaking down as he delivered her eulogy. I think of the pride and the strain in his voice as he told her assembled family and friends and colleagues, fellow Equity card holders, about all the various strands of her life. I remember that he invited people to applaud her, saying it was the sound that Anne liked the best, and they did. I remember that as Dad stood outside the church following the service, his stiff black coat seemed to be holding him up and that it was smeared with pancake foundation where Nana's stagey friends had embraced him in their grief. I think: if Grace can have that – a theatrical career and a happy marriage and children and so many people at her funeral – then I can rest in peace myself.

Meanwhile, I am working through my own dramas as my running becomes more and more of a challenge.

These days, I am never quite sure which characters I will meet when I run.

I don't mean the passers-by: late commuters turning into their driveways, shoppers alighting at bus stops, dog-walkers and ramblers, allotment gardeners and parents in the swing park.

No, I mean versions of me. Increasingly, I find that I am locked in internal dialogue that is simultaneously enthralling and exhausting as I create this new personality for myself.

Often, when I set off, I have butterflies, a nervous tightening in my stomach and a prickle in the palms of my hands. As I close the garden gate and set my watch to record my time and distance, I wonder: which one of me is doing this run? Will I run it with ease and set a new time? Or will I have to talk myself through every mile? Does triumph await? Or misery?

Almost without fail, the first 3 miles of any run are hard work. While my mind is wiping itself clean of the day's tension and filing notable events away, my body is fighting me. Ugh, here we go again, it tells me. Are you kidding? After the day you've had? Why aren't you on the sofa? As I push on through those first minutes, I am wholly and entirely engaged in psychological games with myself. 'You can do this bit,' I say, as the first hill arrives. 'Hills, pfft, this is nothing. Remember the one on the heath last week? You've done this one hundreds of times now.'

But having done it before is no longer a measure of reassurance. There is so much at stake now. There is so much riding on this. The half-marathon is just weeks away. I have raised around a thousand pounds – a sum that makes me blink with wonder. People are expecting this of me. Grace expects this of me. Failure, as the Hollywood-style voiceover intones in my head every time I run, is not an option. To stop would be disaster. To slow down, a defeat. I am often nauseous with fear and the panicky thrill of second-guessing my own abilities.

One night, after I had finally finished the round of homework, dinner, bath and bed with my daughters, I opened the front door to run and saw it was entirely black outside. It perfectly encapsulated my mood: what I was now engaged in was not the stuff of balmy evenings and soft summer mornings; it had become something darker and more complex. There were struggles here. Something was being forged here.

Even my appearance was changing. I was no longer a middle-aged mum in ill-fitting leisurewear, but a serious runner. Getting ready to leave now meant putting on a costume of long tights, warm long-sleeved athletic tops and reflective jacket. I rarely ran fewer than 6 miles and regularly ran more than ten. I was starting to understand why the language of the running community has such an intense ring: we are warriors, athletes, philosophers. Long-distance running is both a mental and physical challenge and only the fittest survive. I was proud of what I was achieving, and also scared by it. Each time I ran further and faster I wondered at my achievement and frightened myself at the thought that I might not be able to better it.

One Saturday morning, I had to run 12 miles: the furthest I had ever had to run. I set my alarm but awoke before it went off, feeling fretful and uneasy. I ate to fuel my body, gaining no pleasure from the cereal and banana that I struggled to swallow.

I set off and for as long as I could manage, I avoided looking at my watch. I barely glanced at my surroundings or the path that I was following. I was entirely lost in a multi-layered, schizophrenic, mental debate, telling myself I could do this while feigning a light-heartedness – take it easy, stop worrying – that made some of the other me's shrug with annoyance, even as others tried harder to calm my jitters. At 8.5 miles I encountered a hill so steep I could almost have leaned forward to kiss the road before me. I willed myself to keep going, to somehow get one leg in front of the other, again and again, to straighten up and relax my shoulders and suck in big lungfuls of air. A third of the way up, blind panic set in. With nearly 4 miles still to do, I simply couldn't see how I would complete this run. It was like turning over an exam paper to discover that none of the questions corresponded to those I had prepared for: I felt like simultaneously bursting into tears and being sick. Resorting to tiny, staggering granny steps I shambled somehow to the crest and back on to the flat.

The next two and a bit miles were manageable, but I had started to feel pain in my right knee, where I'd fallen by accident a couple of weeks earlier. It gradually got worse and worse. By 11 miles, I had shooting pains the entire length of my right leg, from groin to instep. Every step made me grit my teeth and close my eyes.

I have no idea how I completed that last mile. Putting the key into my front door was like coming round after a period of unconsciousness. I was shaking. Climbing the stairs to the bathroom took me ten minutes. I ran a bath and sat on the floor watching the bubbles form, aware of every tendon and joint in my body. I was still on the edge of tears as I struggled to undress. Somehow, I hauled myself into the bath and sank below the lavender foam, feeling it pop in my ears and float through my hair as the blessed heat of the water soothed my muscles.

When I came up for air, I was grinning. It was like hearing applause.

8

Restore, revive

It's a Sunday evening and I have spent the day trying to ignore a growing hangover, the result of a slightly overexcited dinner with a friend last night. My eyeballs feel like they have been sandpapered; my bloated stomach murmurs sourly. I have the tail end of a cold. I'm shattered.

Finally, the girls are in bed. Everyone's Monday morning clothes are laundered, dinner has been made, eaten, cleared away. I have checked my emails and my diary, made my latest to-do list and selected my own outfit for the morning, which lies ready for me to dress quickly and quietly in the dark tomorrow, to tiptoe away towards the train before dawn.

But now, I have just placed a clean, fluffy towel on to the bathroom radiator, beside my book. The bath water is hot, and scented with rosemary and eucalyptus. I sink into it, groaning: and the bathroom door opens.

'Can I tell you about that thing I made up today, Mummy?' asks Grace from the doorway.

I cannot bring myself to say no, go back to bed – so I nod tiredly and she comes in and sits cross-legged on the bath mat beside me and starts to tell me a story. I lie back and feel the hot water wash over my shoulders. I breathe out and tell myself to relax. Let her talk. The day is done. There are no impediments. Let her talk.

So I lie and listen and Grace talks. It's a funny story, the narrative very detailed, if sometimes lacking in explanation regarding the colourful and surprising plot.

Ten minutes later I need to rinse my hair. I tell Grace to hold on a minute because I won't be able to hear her, and I close my eyes and submerge my head.

Underwater, I can make out her muffled tones continuing on. With my head still beneath the suds, I raise my hands up out of the water in mock surrender. Above me I feel her still-little fingers close over mine and fit into their accustomed hold as Grace continues with her story. When I emerge again, we are still holding hands and she pauses briefly to say, 'That looked really nice, when you were floating under the water,' then she continues again. I daub myself with a gooey face mask which makes her giggle and ask to try some. Then she is momentarily diverted by the smell of the eucalyptus and asks me a series of questions about it. But mostly, throughout the thirty minutes I had allotted myself for my bath and relaxation before bed, Grace keeps me company and keeps talking.

I am not the only one of us, I think, who finds it hard to capture enough time for nourishing rest. Grace struggles to get to sleep most nights, finding it difficult to switch off and sometimes, I think, to physically close her eyes – hence her adoption of one of my eye masks, discovered during an illicit exploration of my bedroom drawers. In the course of changing her bed sheets I often find torches, books, notepads and a wide selection of toys. I realised years ago that there was no point telling her off about this: the process of lying still and waiting for sleep can wind her up to such a degree that confiscating her playthings is often counter-productive. I have been lucky in that she has always been happy enough to go to bed – even when she was a baby I was able to establish a routine that meant I could put her down awake after her last feed and she would kick and sing to herself and watch her mobile for as long as it took her to nod off.

These days the time when Grace can really relax is during the holidays, when she is freed from the trauma of homework and high-pressure classroom situations, the torture of school-yard etiquette and the bone-sapping effort required just to navigate the duties and expectations of each day.

As I write this part now, Grace is on holiday with her dad for two weeks.

The house is very quiet.

I think of her running along beaches with salt in her hair and sand in her fingernails, singing to mermaids and sea-gulls, and I smile.

The last two days we spent together she was shipwrecked and dripping after a stormy term at school, and in need of resuscitation. The more tired she becomes the further away from me she drifts. On the last morning of school I sent her upstairs to get her blazer from her wardrobe and put it on. Ten minutes later, she trailed dreamily back like Ophelia, murmuring tall tales and music to herself with all thoughts of her original task forgotten. That same evening I found her cleaning her teeth in the shower, chewing her brush and rearranging shampoo bottles with an unfocused gaze. I helped her out of the stall and wrung out her socks.

Now that she is literally gone – across the sea to Ireland – I miss her. But I know the damp air and misty fairy tales of her fatherland will bring her home to me renewed: a mischievous sprite with dancing eyes and roses in her cheeks.

In preparation for her return I must reinvigorate myself. It's only now, sitting at my desk with baby Betty playing by my feet, that I register how tired I am too. I am exhausted. Knackered. Wrung out, done for, banjaxed. Fatigued. Frayed. I could sleep for a fortnight and still not wake.

This is not an option, however. I must run instead, as the days to the half-marathon tick down inexorably. And I must be bright and strong when Grace returns.

In preparation for the race I have been steadily building up my mileage week by week. I have discovered with amazed joy the exceptional things my body can do when I ask.

I ran 8 miles, with knees that felt like glass.

I ran 9 miles, several of them in torrential rain.

I ran 10 miles, selecting a route that took me straight up a soul-destroying hill.

I had not anticipated the massive highs of such an accomplishment. Nor had I anticipated how floored I would be by this level of physical activity on top of my daily routine.

So I sought professional advice and, via the National Register of Personal Trainers, found Amelia Watts, endurance runner and marathon trainer extraordinaire. Amelia can run seven marathons in seven days in seven counties. Soon she will run the Marathon des Sables, across the Sahara desert in Morocco. Amelia could have my half-marathon for breakfast. Actually, she could have it for pre-breakfast, and be picking it out of her teeth before sunrise.

Amelia came to visit me and assess my body's fitness for endurance. She is a long blonde sinew. I am a tired forty-year-old. After a battery of tests, Amelia concluded that I have good balance and blood pressure and breathing. (Not bad, given that I only stopped a twenty-year cigarette habit six months ago.) But my core strength is sadly lacking. The muscles that hold me together deep inside need some serious work. At times over this last year I felt like I was falling apart. Now I know why.

But I also know that I can mend myself while I work to make things better for Grace. Amelia devised a schedule that included mileage and also strength training and stretching, to renovate my poor, twice-Caesareaned stomach and improve the flexibility of muscles in my neck and shoulders and back which had become shortened and stiff. I shuddered inwardly when I saw the plans she had laid out for me: for starters, I had to buy a giant plastic ball (upon which I then had to lie and do sit-ups – twice the exertion, given the effort of balancing involved) and a studded length of foam, which I was required to roll up and down my calves and thighs post-run (the pain of this was surprising and excruciating).

It was no longer enough to just fall out of the house and run. I had to condition myself from head to foot. Once again, I realised that my life had changed entirely with Grace's diagnosis. It felt like a series of slaps. After each blow, I would shake my head to clear it and think – aha, this is what I must do – only to find again, a short while later, that it was only the latest task, only a part of the challenge that now lies ahead of me.

Even asking for help was a constant, ongoing process: tiring and time-consuming and I consistently failed to realise that this was now my life, that the process of asking for help that never quite came soon enough would be an ongoing battle.

At first, outside of pushing for more information for Grace, of speeding up the diagnosis then asking for educational aid, I didn't think about seeking support from anywhere else. The running was everything. It was easier to keep all my concerns inside and rely on long, silent runs to beat them into submission: just the thought of starting to tell someone what I was facing and doing exhausted me. There was so very, very much of it and it was so discouraging. It was easier to drag it around with me, tombstone-heavy, than attempt to lift it up for someone else to see.

And anyway, who would I tell? And what would they say if I did tell them?

'When I got my son's diagnosis, I suddenly realised I had no one to phone,' said my friend Sam. 'My "mummy" friends – the ones that see you through weaning, breastfeeding and the rest – didn't have any experience of this. We lost friends, people drifted away because they found Nathan's behaviour too difficult.'

I had my family to talk to, of course. My mum and dad, both still teaching and working, who would always drop what they were doing to talk to me, always available and always comforting. My sisters, who would hug me and make me laugh. My patient husband, who saw first-hand my distress and that of Grace, whom he loved dearly, despite spending the first few years of his relationship with her dodging her kicks and punches. (He was funny, and she would laugh at his silliness, and then feel guilty for laughing and enjoying his company because he wasn't her dad.)

But still, somehow, I would talk to them and feel lonely. It was like standing on an island and calling out to passing ships.

One day I came home from a run and found myself crying under the shower and realised that I wasn't holding together very well any more, regardless of the number of miles or sit-ups I did. The National Autistic Society seemed like the most obvious place to go first for help. They would know exactly how I was feeling and they would know how to make it better, I was sure.

I called the NAS helpline, aware of a sensation like holding my breath. The number rang briefly and then switched to music. Shortly afterwards a recording of a young-sounding, politely female voice advised me that all the lines were engaged and asked me to call back, or leave my name and address should I wish to receive an information pack.

If only there was an information pack on how to stop crying. I sat and leaked tears for a long time that day, trying the number again and again and finding it always busy.

'At the moment we can't meet demand and we do really struggle,' Emma Delaney, NAS helpline manager for the last four years, told me when we talked later. 'Our at-risk calls have increased a lot lately. We have a lot of people who are very distressed because of the financial situation and difficult work environment. People seem very desperate.'

Emma explained that aside from people with autism themselves, a lot of parents approach the NAS, feeling isolated, having just got the diagnosis and been left to get on with it. She said that the NAS will talk them through the main issues and look for support groups in their area. She also mentioned a parent-to-parent group which provides emotional support.

So I looked up the parent-to-parent group. I filled in a form online asking if someone could please call me and left details of the times I was free for a volunteer to ring me back.

Nothing happened. Then I rang the parent-to-parent helpline number and left my details there. A week, two weeks passed. Still nothing happened. By now I felt like I was crawling through the days, assault-course style; covered in mud and gritting my teeth but still going, despite wondering how I was going to climb the wall I knew was up next.

Grace was still friendless and often sad about it. The battle to get her diagnosis recognised by the local education authority was still ongoing. Her teachers were helpful sometimes.

There was a lot more Grace needed and I was running out

of emotional reserves. She was starting to notice me crying when she cried.

I did some more research and found a number for a local autism support group. I phoned that number four times. Each time it was dead. I found another number and rang that. A woman answered and said hello. I asked her if she could help me find a local parents' support group and a club that my daughter could go to in order to meet other children with Aspergers and feel less lonely. The woman sounded doubtful. No, she said, we don't really do very much like that. I can put you in touch with some other groups, but you have to have a statement to be allowed to use them. Does your child have a statement of educational needs? No, I said. Oh well, she said.

Another week passed. Daily, I felt more brittle. I went to work, I ran, I hugged Grace a lot and said reassuring things. Betty went through a phase of not sleeping and so I got up two or three times a night to settle her.

I kept looking and emailing anyone I thought might help.

A little while later, one of Grace's doctors gave me the phone number of a woman who ran a local group. This time it was good news.

Yes, she said brightly, we meet once a week. There's an opportunity to talk to other parents, you can bring your daughter to meet other kids with Aspergers. There are computers for them, and an art room. And we run social-skills classes that she's welcome to join in with, if she feels like it. You've got a little one? Don't worry, there are lots of siblings there too and people to volunteer to come and help out.

I thought I might faint with relief and said so. I could hear the woman smile down the phone at me. She gave me an address and a time and said she'd be waiting outside to take us in and introduce us to everyone.

In the days that followed I felt sure I'd cracked it. Grace was perky at the prospect of meeting new friends; and for me, the chance to sit down in a group of mothers who would know the details of my life felt like preparing for a visit to old acquaintances.

As Sophie's mum Nic said: 'Local groups have been a life-saver for us. We meet once a month and it's been so nice to talk to other parents of autistic children. Sometimes you think you're going mad: your child is always talking to themselves in the mirror, or asking for help drying themselves after the bath because they can't use a towel. It's so nice to talk to other parents who completely understand where you're coming from and who know how you feel.'

Sam agreed: 'It wasn't until I was meeting other parents in the same boat that I felt supported at all. We've made friends who have autistic kids, and you can be normal and know that no one's judging you.'

But the moment I walked into that group I thought: I don't want to be here.

We were in a block of classrooms at the local boys' school. The neon strip lights overhead were so bright they made my tired eyes feel even more dusty and baggy. It was like walking on to a pitch under floodlights: I felt exposed and naked in the merciless light and unsure what game I was playing.

We were shown around, Betty trotting at my side and

Grace trailing slightly behind. At the end of a corridor were two rooms full of boys on computers. Grace put her face to the rectangle of glass in the door to see in and turned to shoot a look of request over her shoulder at me. I nodded and she went in, sat down at an empty cubicle and started pointing and clicking with the mouse. With Grace installed, Betty turned and set off at a fast jog down the corridor back to the room where mums were eating biscuits and drinking tea. In a small circle of chairs around spindly-legged grey institutional tables, a group of women were taking it in turns to say how bad their child's level of education and support was. Every one of them looked tired, many wearing clothes that looked thrown together and an expression of battle-weariness, the exhaustion of their children's lives on their shoulders. I froze.

As I turned to look for Betty I caught a glimpse of my own reflection in the classroom windows. I looked haggard and unkempt, dressed in the jumble of garments I had dragged on unthinkingly that morning. I looked worse than everyone else. I went over and sat down.

Someone made me a cup of tea and put it into my hand. The thread of conversation wound around and around me, tighter and tighter. Someone's son had been given a book about social skills and left alone to read it. Someone else's son had not received any physical therapy for weeks, despite endless phone calls and requests. Under the lights everyone's faces looked bleached.

Betty saved me, tugging at my clothes until I rose and took her over to the furthest corner and a desk set up with

Play-Doh and cutting-out shapes. Every time I thought she was settled I half-rose to go back to the group, but I couldn't quite do it and she squawked in protest whenever I moved.

After a while someone came over and smiled and sat down. She asked me about my daughter and I told her briefly about my concerns. She talked to me about her son and the kind of other activities I could consider for Grace.

'The Scouts are good,' the woman said. 'They do take disabled ones.' And she nodded kindly and reassuringly at me.

At that moment Betty sprinted off again. I got up to see where she had gone.

'We've got her, you know,' the woman said, inclining her head in the direction that my toddler had taken. 'That's why there are so many adults and supervisors. So you can sit.'

I faked a laugh and said: 'So I'm fretting too much?'

'Yes,' said my companion. She scribbled her phone number on a piece of paper and pushed it across to me. She smiled again and said nothing. I took it and felt tears welling and blinked hard rapidly, and went to check on Betty anyway.

I found her in the computer room with Grace and the boys. There were lots of boys. Some were little. Lots were hulking, hunch-shouldered, awkward adolescents made more gauche by their condition. They sat in rows in front of screens, shooting things. A couple stood in clumsy knots in the corner having mumbled conversations. Among them Grace sat neatly, silently, her face an unreadable blank, her eyes big and solemn as she looked at her computer. She had configured her screen into a television and was watching episodes of her favourite BBC programme.

On the way home Grace said: 'That was cool, when can we go again?'

I didn't know what to say. I didn't know what there was for her to find cool and suspected that really she had just enjoyed not having to go home and do her piano practice.

I said: 'Did you meet anyone? Or talk to anyone?'

She said, 'No.' A little while later as we walked through darkening streets, she told me how lonely she felt.

That night Grace's dad came to pick her up for the evening. After they left, I sat down on the sofa and thought about the events of the afternoon. Suddenly I was crying – huge storms that shook my shoulders as tears rained down on to my lap. I sobbed and sobbed until I was a snotty mess, drops hanging from my nose that I wiped inelegantly away with the heels of my hands.

I thought: I am a horrible snob. I don't want to take her back to that club because I don't want to be one of those mums. I thought: I don't want to take her back because I don't want that for my daughter. She is not disabled. She is not the class square. She is not a maths geek who can find his fit with science-club friends and superlative numbers skills and computer classes. She is different. She is elegant and funny and sassy. She is not normal. I want more for her. I am a terrible mother. I am making this about me.

I thought: maybe she just needs to know that she's not on her own. Maybe we should go back and try again next week.

As I sat on the sofa and snivelled, my phone rang. I picked it up. A soft voice asked if I was Sophie and introduced herself. She said she was calling from the National Autistic Society's parent-to-parent line. I sagged, letting myself fall a little, and at once wailed even louder. She made soothing noises until, between gasps, I managed to thank her for calling and told her about my day.

'I feel like I've let my daughter down again,' I said. 'I wish she didn't have to feel so alone all the time. I don't know how to fix this. I do what I can for her at school: at least there's a process, however head-bangingly slow and frustrating, that I can follow to get her some help. But for friendship, there's nothing I can do. I keep phoning all these numbers and emailing all these people and I still can't find her a friend. Just one friend . . . '

And I was off again. By this time I was crying so hard that my nose had ballooned and when I spoke I sounded as though I was choking on wasps.

The woman at the other end of the phone was unperturbed. Calmly, caringly, she said: 'You sound like you're standing in a room with all these doors and every time you knock on one it just stays closed.' While I blew my nose, she told me about her son, who is autistic, and how she felt isolated and sad because no one wanted to be with him. She told me she knew how I felt.

'It's so undignified,' I wept. 'She's not a charity case. She's lovely. She just never gets to show it. There seems to be an inherent loneliness in her condition. I can't seem to find her the right – the right – f-f—i-i-t . . . ' The crying took me over again and I couldn't talk for a while.

The woman on the other end of the phone asked me gently

about my daughter and I calmed down as I talked to her about Grace.

After a while, she told me: 'She sounds wonderful and she sounds like she has a lovely time with you. It's very hard. But you have each other.'

And she told me: 'You sound like an amazing mum. You also sound very tired and like you need a break.'

The woman on the other end of the phone made some suggestions. She directed me to some Facebook groups for parents of children with Aspergers. She told me the names of some online forums. She suggested that I ask around for other parents of girls with Aspergers. Perhaps I could find her a pen-friend.

As she talked, I made a list. I realised as I was doing it that I was coming out of this advice session with another list. But I felt less lonely.

The next morning Grace had an appointment with her counsellor. I drove her to the health centre and took her in and then sat in the waiting room outside, looking about me at yet more utility chic. I reflected on the fact that I had now spent so much time in these sorts of places that I was beginning to compile a furniture catalogue for local authority institutions in my head. Green chairs – check. Linoleum with a mosaic pattern – check. Formica-topped coffee table – check. Wall pictures – check. At least one of them a seascape or dawn scene – check. This room had one that combined both – double check.

As Grace walked away with her counsellor, she looked suddenly very soft and little, her posture betraying her uncertainty. Feeling a knot start to harden in my throat, I focused on the picture opposite me as a way of gathering my thoughts. And finally, I understood why these places always have calmingly anodyne pictures of sunrises and sunsets and beaches. Taking deep breaths, I concentrated on every detail: the white-grained sand churned with footprints; the foamy, lace-edged waves; the yellow–orange sunburst reflected across the horizon line; and the intricate pattern of clouds swirling across the sky.

It helped for a while.

Then I got up to go to the ladies' room to splash water on my face, and the act of moving broke my composure. I stood in the toilets crying. Bloody, bloody, bloody *hell*. This should be progress, I thought. Grace is getting help. But all I could feel was frightened for her, worried about her state of mind and scared about the impact of these endless interventions, the push and shove of school, the round of questioning physicians and the latest hare-brained scheme that her hopeless mother had subjected her to.

Somehow I had to stop the tears. I was starting to bore myself with the weight of my worries. I would keep talking to people. I'd go back to the support group and ask if anyone knew of any girls around Grace's age with Aspergers. I'd sign up to the various online groups and post messages about pen-friends. Hell, I'd offer up my own kitchen and tea supply, if I could find some other mothers to join me in an 'Aspergirls' group.

I spoke to my doctor and asked about resources. I accepted another list of autism-related organisations. I allowed myself to be bargained into accepting another prescription for more antidepressants, but thought I would leave it in my coat pocket for a little while until I'd decided whether I wanted them. I filled in a questionnaire about the extent of my depression. And I agreed to go back in a few weeks.

That night I ran. I went to the gym, seeking bright lights and company and noise. While groups of balloon-shouldered muscle men stood in groups clanking weights and grunting encouragement to one another, I ran. As women in tiny yoga vests gossiped around the water cooler, I ran. Behind me, people got on and off the stationary bikes and the rowing machines. Still I ran. I wondered how much money I would raise in total by completing the half-marathon and I wondered how much of my money would go towards helping to keep that NAS advice line open. I thought of the woman who phoned me and the other parents like her. I wondered what they did when they put down the phone to people like me. I wondered who helped them. And I kept running. And after a while I stopped thinking and just listened to the beat of my pulse in my ears telling me I was still here and still going.

9

Happy families

That summer, we spent the holidays in Normandy and fought more battles.

The enemy approached across a lush landscape of orchards and cornfields. Wave after relentless wave of rain bore down on us, drumming through clustered stone hamlets and lashing hedgerows and lanes.

In the face of such a deluge, we sought many and varied strategies, tilting at one idea after another and fighting down panic. We began with straight confrontation: on the first day of our holiday we put on our armour and clad in anoraks and sensible shoes marched past the pool and sun loungers to find other entertainment. We went to Avranches, explored the cathedral and perused the botanical gardens under lowering skies. We admired the Mont St Michel, shimmering in the distance across the bay, tethered by a silver ribbon of river across the mudflats. Then we went home and dried off.

The next day we tried ignoring the bombardment. The

kids gamely unpacked toys and played in the sitting room of our cottage, marching Lego figures across decorative rugs and carved occasional tables whose every sharp corner was a reminder how much nicer it would be to be outdoors. The bickering began. In a sinister twist, the game was renamed Lego Riots. Hastily, we made sandwiches and put everyone into the car for a trip to picturesque Villedieu-les-Poeles, famed for its copper pots and pans. We walked through the market, bought sausages and cooed over fluffy ducklings in crates until Betty, wrinkling her nose at the animal smell, urged us on.

The drizzle was low-level but building, as was the bickering. I slipped away into a gift shop and bought ceramic bowls painted with figures in regional dress and finished with our names in flourishing Gallic script. I willed us to be a happy family as I watched the shop assistant stack and wrap and bind us in protective bubble-wrap.

At lunchtime we hid out like maquis in the massive, silent Forest of Saint Sever. My husband carved up sausage and handed around bread to dejected troops as huge raindrops plopped on to us from the canopy above.

By now Grace was retreating further into herself, irritated by any request or interruption to her internal stream of thought in the absence of any compelling external activity. My younger stepson D, bruised by Grace's bluntness and tired of playing nice, was a tinder box in the dampness. J, my elder stepson, alternately teased the others and then retreated aloof behind his *Beast Quest* books. The in-fighting started in earnest.

This was not the holiday I'd longed for. This was not the giggling bonding with Grace in the pool under the sun, dipping and ducking and twisting to catch her ankles in the turquoise blue. This was not lazy and relaxed. Our cottage smelled increasingly damp and sour with boredom and disappointment.

The next day the boys insisted it wasn't really raining and lobbed a tennis ball disconsolately back and forth in the wet garden, then played half-hearted games of Monopoly before falling out. Grace circled and paced. She hates ball games requiring co-ordination and loathes board games using numbers and other people's rules. She could not settle to read. Even drawing could not hold and soothe her. All she could think of was when or whether she would next be able to get into the swimming pool. She asked me over and over and over. By nine-thirty one morning I found myself counting the hours until dinner when I could have a drink.

On day five, we tried another tactic – outrunning the rain. We drove for an hour flanked by dark clouds, then suddenly pulled free of them. A cheer went up in the car. We found Fougères, a charming medieval town laid out on different levels like a game of snakes and ladders, with steps leading to dead ends and turnings that brought us back to where we started. And then there was the castle: a giant ring of crenellated fortress walls dotted with wild flowers and strung with piebald turrets from which the children chased bats.

By evening the enemy had found us again and the rain came all night like handfuls of needles thrown at our windows. The next day we surrendered entirely and sat watching the miles of rain clouds that stretched in every direction. The kids refused to get in the car, but gave up asking if they might be able to swim. My husband and I defused quarrel after row after scratchy argument. My heart was in my boots. I had set such store by this time together with no homework and no chores and no work stress. But Grace was as detached as ever, furious and cutting whenever I asked her to take part in tedious family routines and no closer to the boys who could barely be in the same room themselves for five minutes before locking horns.

I tried to get away and run, but could only manage a short, slow slog, hampered by rain and hills and a lack of form after a recent virus. I am rubbish at everything, I wheezed to myself.

Back at the cottage, as I started to think about what I should begin to pack first, the sky began to brighten. I ignored it. But then the sun came out – tentatively, like it knew it was in trouble – and we all rushed outside, turning our faces up to it like sunflowers. The cheering warmth was divine. We scurried to the pool, where Grace, J and D leaped in with whoops and splashes and started to shove each other around like old comrades. My husband bobbed gently around the shallow end with Betty, beaming, fastened around his neck. Like atoms, my family spun and bounced and separated and then clustered together in the middle of the pool, arms around each other, hugging and kissing while I watched from the side with a lump in my throat.

Within thirty minutes it was raining again. But this time

the sun remained, stubbornly undimmed. We ate dinner with all the doors and windows open, beneath a rainbow.

Grace's new school year started well. She looked relaxed and happy in the first days of term when I went to collect her: striding out of the classroom on long, tawny legs and flicking hair out of her eyes with the self-assurance of a sixteen-year-old. A school trip away – three whole nights at an outdoors activity centre – turned out to be a huge success. While I fretted and paced (and ran), Grace scaled treetops and swam lengths and filmed a bunch of lopsided, giggly dorm videos of herself and friends. Once back in school routine, her first maths classes passed smoothly – a major accomplishment for her – and she established a pattern of playing with two or three classmates in rotation at break, an arrangement that meant she had a willing accomplice for her repetitive games every interval.

But the next hurdle had already appeared, much closer to home this time.

One evening after work, I went to collect my children: first to school, then, with Grace chatting easily beside me in the car, I parked outside the home of Betty's childminder and right on cue, my toddler ran outside, splendid in her pink hoody, baggy jeans and sparkly trainers. I jumped out to get her. Betty paused on the path, her white-blonde hair caught in a sudden breeze. She was scanning the car. When she spotted Grace her shoulders slumped.

'No, Cee-Cee,' Betty said, and turned back to her childminder. I intercepted her deftly, scooped her up and kissed her. I told her hello and that I had missed her and not to be silly. I told her lovely Gracie had missed her too. 'No, Cee-Cee,' she said again, but this time she sounded resigned. I took her over to the car and opened the door and put her into her car seat and buckled her in, saying brightly, 'Hello, Cee-Cee!' for her. Grace smiled, tentatively. Betty looked at her shoes and said, 'Hello, Cee-Cee,' in a tiny voice.

Back home, Grace announced that she was going to do her piano practice and disappeared into the front room. Betty pottered and chattered while I cooked, bringing bits and pieces of coloured plastic for me to admire and occasionally giving a brisk tug on my trousers to express her impatience for food. The meal was soon ready and I asked her to go and tell Grace to come and get her tea. She wouldn't. I asked again. She took a few steps, then stood silently with her back to me. I asked her three times, to no response, then said sharply: 'Please do as you are told.' She ran into the front room and let fly a barrage of angry noise, nearly-words expressing fury at Grace, who, in turn, burst into the kitchen like a bat out of hell, tears streaming, to shriek at me: 'I can't take any more! I'm sick of this! She hates me!'

I scolded Betty, who burst into tears and buried her face in my legs, and tried to soothe Grace, who was entwined around my arm and neck, still wailing. I shuffled over to the dinner table, making soothing noises, and somehow sat them both down. They were quickly distracted by the food I had placed ready for them and started to eat. After a pause, Betty began to chatter again and to try to tell me about her day. 'Man,' she began. 'Grandma man.' She got no further. Grace exploded into laughter and pointed at her, exclaiming how funny her lack of words made her sound. Betty knitted her brows and frowned deeply at Grace, hurt and cross. Grace was oblivious. She threw her head back and laughed and laughed. I asked her to be quiet and explained how Betty might be feeling as she struggled to express herself.

Betty tried again. Grace set off laughing again. Betty was beside herself with irritation and the effort of making herself understood and started to yell at Grace again. I counted to ten in my mind, dampening down the urge to raise my voice and wondered guiltily if Betty was taking her cue from me, given how often I shouted at her big sister myself.

After the girls had eaten Grace went off again to finish her music. As I stacked the dishwasher, Betty trotted over to me.

'Worried,' she said, and frowned again.

I closed the dishwasher door and clicked it shut and said: 'Why?'

'Baby,' she said simply and I sat on the floor so that she could clamber into my arms and be rocked. With her head in the crook of one of my elbows and her ankles crossed in the other, she nibbled a biscuit and gazed up at me. Behind my back I could feel the warmth and hum and occasional clank of our plates being rinsed by the dishwasher.

'Are you OK?' I asked Betty, and stroked her little ear.

She burrowed further into my arms and nibbled one of them experimentally, grazing it with her baby teeth. 'Worried,' she said again, conversationally.

'Don't be,' I told her. 'I love you.'

She looked up at me again, with her father's startling blue eyes, and said: 'Too, Mummy.'

Later, as we prepared to go upstairs for her bath, I asked her to go and say goodnight to her sister, who was watching a film. Betty ran to Grace on the sofa and kissed her with a loud smack. Grace, delighted, immediately asked her: 'Do you love me, Betty? Do you? Do you?'

Betty didn't answer, but ran away, casting a naughty smile over her shoulder. Grace threw a cushion after her in mock frustration. Then she turned contentedly back to the television.

Meanwhile, the running was teaching me too about unforeseen challenges, particularly the art of endurance, which I increasingly found was more about my mind than my muscles. Coasting out one Saturday morning for what I expected to find an easy session, I was appalled to find it wasn't and that I was going to have to rely on mental strength to see me through it.

Get me. A rough morning's run and I turned into Papillon.

Clearly, 7 miles through the nature reserve and gated communities of footballing millionaires in tidy Barnet is not sufferance, and once I was back to sitting on my sofa with a cup of tea and only moderately aching legs I could see that. But at nine o' clock, earlier that morning, mud-splattered and winded, I was locked in a form of solitary confinement that was as close to despair as anything I had so far experienced. (At this point I am resisting the temptation to draw parallels between the life of a working mum and that of a hard-core felon sentenced to hard labour and only limited contact with other adults.)

That day's run was a shortie: a bit of down time between the 10 and 11 miles of previous weeks and the 12- and 13-mile tests that loomed next. In between my long runs I'd been trying to improve my strength and speed: doing lunges and sit-ups that left me purple-faced, alternated with 3-mile dashes that induced such nausea I had to resist the impulse to stop and vomit into the bushes.

A lot of training didn't feel nice. But then some of it suddenly would and I'd be spilling over with purpose and happy chemicals and the certainty that I could be everything Grace needed and that we could together emerge victorious from this marathon.

But, oh God, that run.

It was supposed to be easy. It was supposed to be confirmation of how far I had progressed, how tough my legs and body and core were becoming. Instead it was an awful, shambling progression during which a voice in my head crowed in triumphant dismay that I'd made absolutely no progress at all, that I'd been kidding myself if I thought I could do this. By the time my watch beeped the signal that ended my torment I was nearly in tears. How could I have gone from 11 miles last Saturday, via two mid-week runs totalling 8 miles (and yielding two personal bests), to this?

I racked my brains over and over for the answer but it was unforthcoming and I had to file the incident away, still as bewildered. At times that morning and in the following days I veered into panic about how I would get to the end of those 13 miles on 9 October.

But I didn't have time for further musing – with all the potential damage it could do to my progress so far – because I was diverted by more family squabbles.

Hampering my ability to unravel the fights and the counter-accusations was my constant worry about precisely how I should be dealing with this. I didn't want to baby Grace or make special allowances for her that might aggrieve the others, but at the same time I didn't see how I could expect the same of her as I did of my other children. Keeping an even hand – and an even tone – was proving to be extremely difficult and time and again I felt that I was doing the wrong thing. So very often she would fail in some way to do as I asked and I would find myself saying her name in the exasperated tones of one who has been let down again, only to feel instantly guilty as she turned hurt, uncomprehending eyes upon me.

As one expert – Jo Attree, a clinical psychologist who specialises in treating children with autistic-spectrum disorders – explained to me later, I was making the mistake (classic among parents of autistic children) of thinking that because my daughter had such a large vocabulary she could understand my wishes, when in fact her articulacy belied a very different way of comprehending events.

'The main difficulty parents face is not being aware or understanding how children with Aspergers function,' said Jo. 'AS children tend to be articulate, so parents think they're dealing with more ability than they are. But these children are fundamentally different in the way they interpret the world. It's difficult for parents when they don't know quite what they're dealing with and which, if you're not trained, may easily be misunderstood.'

One afternoon after I'd collected the girls from daycare and school Betty asked me if she could play with her stickers, so I got down her little craft box and set them out for her, along with some paper and pens. I needed to go into the kitchen – just the adjoining room – and cook dinner, so I asked Grace to sit and play with her little sister. Within ten minutes a wail of intense upset and frustration went up from my toddler and I rushed in to see what had happened. Sitting on the floor beside her baby sister, Grace had created a beautiful piece of artwork with all the material I had made available. Betty, unable to access any of the pens or stickers because Grace had commandeered them all, looked up at me with fat tears of indignation swelling in her eyes.

'For goodness sake!' I shouted, hearing a pan of vegetables boil over with hissing, steaming urgency behind me as I hurried forward to redistribute everything. 'I said to play with her, not take everything off her!' Grace hung her head and mumbled something. She looked mortified.

'One thing we hear a lot is: "What have I done?"' said Jo, who counsels families through exactly these kinds of situations. 'You may make a statement that seems straightforward to your other children, when, in fact, you're asking them to read between the lines. You tell your child to go and play with a group of children and he or she will go and grab the toy, or take the ball – they won't be able to read the social cues, but they'll be following your instructions literally.'

The frustration I see in Betty is often mirrored in the behaviour of the boys, though being the patient souls that they are it is rare that they complain. Instead, I see J and D quietly turn away, move with unspoken resolve together to another room in the house, or to the garden, or to a solo computer game. Just once have I ever heard J shout 'I've had enough!' and the frightened contrition on his face – warring with a stubborn desire to let me see his anger – still stays with me. We try to talk about what's happening as it happens but sometimes we don't. And sometimes I get it wrong.

One morning the boys were up first and finished a packet of breakfast cereal between them. When Grace came down half an hour later to find it gone – despite there being others for her to choose from – her fury on finding an empty box when she had wanted precisely that cereal that day was massive. As the boys, barely awake, tried to defend themselves against the insults shattering the calm of that Saturday morning, D turned to me desperately at one point and said: 'But I did ask you if it was OK.' He was right and at the time I had heard him, and not giving any thought to why he might be asking for approval, had absent-mindedly said, 'Sure, go ahead.' Now realising what he meant I said crossly to him: 'But why didn't you say what you meant, if you knew this was going to happen?' – and instantly his shoulders slumped. Somehow, despite Grace's bad behaviour, I'd still managed to put him in the wrong.

Living with different rules for different children is something very familiar to Vikki, who has thirteen-year-old Tom and ten-year-old Ben, who has Aspergers:

'The different rules that apply with Ben and Tom are difficult at times to administer. I never shout at Ben; it only frightens him and makes him feel out of control. I do raise my voice to Tom and have certain expectations of him that I wouldn't apply to Ben. I do explain that they are different and Tom understands that – sometimes!

'Tom really is a wonderful brother. He has so much patience and time for Ben. He is, however, not a complete angel and is now into his teens and finds Ben "getting away with things", as he puts it, hard to handle,' Vikki says.

I worry constantly about whether I'm letting Grace 'get away with things'. So often I have given up halfway through an argument with my dead-set, iron-willed child with an exasperated, 'Oh, all right!' I blush to think of the times when I have said to the boys: 'Please, can we just let Grace do this and it will be your turn next.'

Of course, there are other times when I front it out, ignoring the banging headache and the rising tension and the squeals and drumming feet and slammed doors and yelling that occur when Grace is forced into actions she considers unacceptable. Then I look at the pained expressions of the other children and wonder whether I've just done more harm than good.

Thus I phoned Jo to ask for advice. She counselled sticking to my guns:

'You have to think that you're just a mum. You do what you can do. This is part of the condition. But if we think about breaking patterns of behaviour, we have to think about being consistent. If it's going to be difficult for her to share now, it will be all the more difficult when she's fifteen.'

Kelly, another mum I met when seeking advice, has four children, including her six-and-a-half-year-old autistic son Jack, whose needs regularly have to come before the demands of her other children (Lauren and Charlie aged nine and a half and eight and Olivia, who is three).

'Activities outdoors are probably the hardest thing,' says Kelly. 'My two older children want to go to the park, or go swimming or bowling and that's difficult because I have Jack. He has sensory issues: if there are a lot of people and noise, he doesn't cope well. It can cause him a lot of anxiety and he can flip out. When that happens, he needs to get out and get home to a safe environment. One day, when we all went to the park, I took my eye off Jack for a moment and he disappeared. We lost him for twenty minutes. He had tried to run back home. So I can't go out with all the children without another adult, and that's hard because my husband works six days a week.

'My older children are very good and very patient, but they do get fed up and they do get tired. Lauren has said to me: "I love Jack, but I hate having an autistic brother because we can't do things." She cries when there are things she wants to do and we can't. Quite a lot of the time I say: "I can't do that with you on my own." She has turned around before and said: "It's always about Jack." I feel that all my attention is on Jack and I can't give them what they need. I feel guilty towards my other children because I feel that I'm letting them down.'

I'm very familiar with this feeling. I often feel like I'm letting all of my children down, darting around them and never quite fully catering to any of their needs. With the boys, my relationship – already complicated by being a stepmother – often feels as though it is teetering. For a while, D would ask his dad why it couldn't be like before, when it was just him and his brother and his dad.

'One thing that does help siblings is to validate their feelings,' Jo told me. 'They are expected to grow up quicker than the normal path in life: we expect them to be more patient, kinder. And they do it, but they resent it. They don't realise how hard it is for adults to deal with a child with AS: they just see that that child has to be protected.

'So as much as you can, make it an open topic. It's important for them to feel that they can say they're upset, that they can talk openly about the impact of dealing with this child. Give them space to talk about how upsetting it is or why they feel like this. Tell them: "I can see your point, but I can also tell you that she does not realise how much she annoys you," or, "It is very annoying for you but that's not what she meant, so we need to help her to understand this."'

So I try to explain to the boys the next time a similar incident occurs. I explain that Grace did not intend to cause hurt and that she loves them very much. D hunches his shoulders and angles his body away from me, looking at the floor. J watches me speak, then nods once. So then I redouble my efforts to make them feel better about themselves, and over the next weeks praise them as much as I can. And in so doing I hurt Grace again with my appreciation for, as she sees it, the boys 'being always right'.

What she is referring to is often simply a matter of good behaviour: the boys do as I ask the first time (instead of me having to ask five times and endure lots of 'No!'s from Grace). Sometimes it involves their gentle and affectionate care of

Betty. Grace will observe Betty's behaviour, but not pick up on her cues whereas J will pick up a book to read to Betty when she has become bored of eating and disruptive at meal-times. Or D will take her by the hand and shepherd her to the playhouse in the garden when she tires of the game she is playing and grows fretful. When I say thank you and tell them how helpful they have been, Grace will scowl and sulk. Then I find myself calling on their helpfulness too much.

One night when Grace refused again and again to have a shower, I asked the boys to have one too in order to even things out. J readily agreed so long as he could go first and get it out of the way. Grace immediately insisted on going first, which prompted a row – first with J and then with me – and then a meltdown when I told her off. 'They're all angels and I'm a devil!' she sobbed in the shower as I scrubbed her. 'It makes me feel jealous and sad. It's not fair.'

And just like that, I'm back to square one.

'What you have to acknowledge is that you're not going to achieve this as quickly as you would wish,' Jo explained. 'It's one thing to explain, another to tolerate that your reasoning will take a long time. You just have to do it and do it and do it. Just because your child will understand in one instance doesn't mean they will understand the impact of the actions the next time. You have to always reiterate and repeat. You have to accept the fact that she's going to continue to do it does not mean that you're doing the wrong thing. You explain again. She might learn on that particular occasion, but it doesn't mean she will learn to anticipate. When she makes a hurtful comment she is not saying it to be hurtful.

'These children do learn, they do move on. She's already different from how she was two years ago.'

She's right. It does get better.

One night, Grace learns to make Betty laugh.

It is a Sunday night. Grace is sitting at the dinner table with a scarf wrapped around her head. In front of her is a plate of my finest fish pie, untouched.

Opposite her and down at my side, Betty sits ramrod straight, holding herself tensely in anticipation. Her face, barely peeping over the tabletop, shines with merriment; a tiny giggle, a bubble of glee, escapes from the back of her throat.

My girls are playing.

With a sudden flourish, Grace whips the material away from her face, revealing crazy eyebrows, crossed eyes and lolling tongue. On seeing this, Betty gives a great shout – delighted affirmation – and collapses drunkenly against her seat, so overwhelmed by laughter that she can barely catch her breath.

At this point, I intervene to ask if they will both please eat their food now, before it goes cold. Grace complies. Betty straightens up and reaches for her fork, but her eyes never leave Grace's face. With a stagey sigh, Grace flicks a strand of hair away from her shoulder and eats, but her eyes slide away with a deliberate skittishness that prompts another joyous gurgle from Betty, still watching eagerly for her next move.

Grace spears a piece of broccoli and goggles comically at it. It is all it takes for Betty to explode again into gales that leave her so weak she sags against me, hiccuping, afterwards.

'Come on now, enough,' I say, a bit more firmly this time,

and start spooning food into Betty, who is still prone and snickering softly beside me.

Grace protests: 'What? I didn't do anything!' but then breaks into a wide smile.

In the brief stillness, we all get on with the business of eating. Candles flicker on the table, the fire crackles in the sitting room behind us. Our reflections are ghostly dim in the subdued light, in the kitchen windows, splattered with rain from the storm outside. Across from me my husband catches my eye and smiles as he lifts his glass to drink.

My girls are playing and it brings me such pleasure that I hardly care, really, how much they eat, or whether they finish the meal at all. Hostilities have ceased. Grace has discovered that she can make Betty laugh. She has discovered how to watch her, to read her mood and coax those lovely noises of baby joy from her. Betty has discovered a clown, a tumbling jester behind her sister's often stern countenance. Suddenly the possibilities for revels seem limitless.

Once Betty's hiccups have abated, we move on to cake. Grace tells me a story as she eats, sketching out a scene between two of her latest imaginary characters. But as she talks, she draws everyone in: twinkling at Betty and her stepfather beside her, drawing gestures in the air and turning to us all to see what we think. She is holding court, but she is entirely aware of all of us and taking her cues from our reactions. She smiles at Betty and sees her excitement as the little girl grins up at her, icing smeared across her chin. She smiles at me, and sees my enjoyment of her story warring with concern that she finishes her meal.

As soon as they have cleared their plates and I have acknowledged their request to get down, Betty slips off her chair and trots – pat, pat, pat in her slippers – around to Grace's side.

'C'mon, Cee-Cee,' she says, and holds out her hand. Grace takes it and together they scurry into the sitting room. Just as they disappear from view I catch Grace executing a perfect pantomine pratfall on to the sofa, collapsing with an 'Urgh!' that provokes an explosive guffaw from Betty.

So little, and yet so, so much. It is nothing. It is everything.

10

The Royal Parks

Part One

I'd woken with sweaty palms and a jittery stomach, struggling to remember what was approaching to make me so nervous.

That morning the baby didn't rouse me, nor did my alarm. I lay under the duvet, looking up at the fingers of pale light along the edges of my bedroom curtains and slowly remembering that I didn't have to get up. I didn't have to do a long run that day. I had to rest.

The race was tomorrow. The 13.1-mile Royal Parks half-marathon, winding through the capital city's most beautiful green spaces – expected to be thronged with thousands of observers, supporters and sponsors – in which I was due to participate.

Oh God. I swallowed down a sudden blockage in my throat. I felt as though I was preparing to go on a date with someone I really, really liked: the anticipation was overwhelming, as was the worry things might not turn out the way I'd hoped. I tried to reassure myself. All the signs were that it would be great fun, if occasionally awkward or effortful. I kept having to bat away self-deprecatory imaginings: what if we don't get on? What if all my preparation was in vain? What if I have spectacularly misjudged this and the whole thing is a total disaster?

My mouth was dry. I flung the covers off and went to the kitchen to make coffee.

Downstairs, I counted out spoonfuls of dark brown powder and waited for the kettle to boil, half-listening to the rolling water and tapping my fingers on the counter as my thoughts turned. Of all the mornings in the world not to be running, this was the very worst. Now, more than ever, I needed the soothing anaesthetic of a steady pace, a thumping heart; the back-and-forth piston of my arms and the sound of my own breathing loud in my ears. I needed to be distracted by physical effort to shut down this noise in my head.

I poured the coffee and sipped and paced. In my skittish state, the hot, bitter liquid went straight through me and I had to bolt for the bathroom. I found I was actually trembling.

From upstairs came the sound of baby Betty waking up. I hurried to prepare the breakfast things, glancing up and out of the window as I did so. The grey sky looked back at me neutrally. There were no birds, no neighbourhood cats stalking through the bushes. Even next door's rag-tag bunch of kids were still indoors and silent. The suggestion of a breeze lifted one or two leaves on the willow tree. I was aware of an intense feeling of anticipation. Even the garden seemed to be holding its breath.

Breaking the silence, my phone pinged with another good-luck message from a friend. I muttered ungraciously under my breath. I wish I hadn't told anyone now, I thought, blatantly ignoring the nonsense of this. (The kindness and generosity of my friends and family meant the National Autistic Society would reap more than £2000 if I crossed the finish line on Sunday.) If only nobody knew what I was up to and I could slope off and do this thing with no expectations, I wished.

Then another thought – what on earth was I going to wear? The recent heatwave had passed, thank goodness, but it was not entirely clear whether autumn had properly arrived either. I scrolled feverishly through weather forecasts, which mentioned a cool start, a warmer morning, possibly rain, possibly winds. Layers? A hat? Never had my wardrobe caused me such anxiety – except perhaps for the last big date I went on, which happened almost exactly four years ago and resulted in the discovery of the biggest love of my life.

Thinking about this I brightened and straightened my shoulders. I'm a good judge of character, I told myself. This may be the first time I've done this, but I've been around the block enough times to know when I'm on to a good idea.

And besides, how many dates involve thousands of spectators cheering you on?

Part Two

The next day I opened my eyes at 5.30 a.m. and heard rain pelting down in the darkness outside. Every possible cliché went through my mind: was I tough enough? Was I brave enough? Was I completely mad?

After so many months of training, I would find out what I was really made of. It felt like being sixteen again and waking on the morning of my first exams: the performance I put in over the next few hours had the potential to change the rest of my life completely. Nine months ago I was lost and broken: flattened by the circumstances of my life to such an extent that my doctor was using words like 'depression' and 'nervous breakdown'. Now, having mapped out a route back to sanity and purpose, to looking after Grace and looking after myself, I had to travel the toughest part of the journey so far.

And I had to do it alone. I planned to leave well ahead of the rest of my family and see them later by the side of the route. I wanted to be alone in my final preparations. I shivered, got up and got ready.

Before departing, I looked into Grace's room to say goodbye. Her hair was fanned out on her pillow; her duvet a tangle of knots. Against the noises from the rest of the house that signalled it would soon be time to rise, she clung tightly to sleep. I went to her and kissed her eyelids gently and she murmured: 'Please run slowly, Mummy, because when you're finished and we come back, I've got to do my homework.'

Downstairs, as I stood by the front door, Betty bounced up to me in her pink sleepsuit, her hair a wild mess, chuckling. 'Runrun, Mummy!' she exclaimed, pointing at my now-familiar weekend sports clothing. 'Runrun!'

On the Tube, the overhead lights were harsh against the

darkness of early morning. Some way down the carriage sat a grumpy-looking man in a tiger suit, pretending to look at a map of the race, betrayed in his small piece of theatre by the nervous flicker of his eyes. My running partner Karen and I sat side by side, swaying with the motion of the train, watching him and giggling nervously. I suggested that perhaps his discomfort stemmed from the fact that he'd discovered there was no way to pee while in his suit. Karen thought that perhaps he wasn't running at all, and just liked to go out as a tiger on Sundays. The train nosed deeper and deeper into central London, where more and more runners boarded. By the time we arrived at our final stop, we were all wedged close and starting to perspire: all these participants who had been dutifully hydrating themselves ahead of the race according to sporting advice were now sweating it out instead inside a hot tin can.

Emerging from the Tube station, we saw that outside the sky was steely, though the rain had stopped. We walked and talked nonsense to each other, babbling to cover our nerves, while observing the scene in front of us: crowds of runners converging on the race point, queuing to check bags, to use toilets, to visit the rows and rows of canvas tents that flapped in a cold breeze that brought with it the scent of Deep Heat. We stood on the edge of it all for a moment and watched. Stewards wearing thin plastic anoraks and tangles of coloured lanyards and passes around their necks patrolled the queues for the toilets, braying metallically through megaphones that there were separate urinals for men around the back. About half of the men who were lined up peeled off in grateful relief to look for them. Those still waiting for the stalls coughed and shuffled their feet. A sense of nervous anticipation lay over the scene like mist.

As we made our own preparations, I eyed the crowd. Everyone looked lean and limber. In front of me stood a man wearing a see-through white T-shirt that clung to his every rippling abdominal muscle as he brushed his hands through his Hollywood hairdo and stretched expansively. Beside him stood a golden woman with a long vanilla plait of hair and honey-coloured sinewy legs, who looked like she'd never broken a sweat in her life. My heart started thumping uncomfortably. Where were the reassuringly chunky ones? Where were the runners that looked like mums who ate chocolate? Where were the ones with slightly mottled purple legs and a bit of a wobble round the middle? Oh, God – what had I done?

But then it was time to run. Joining the blue-banded runners aiming for a time somewhere between two and two and a half hours, Karen and I stood shoulder to shoulder in a crowd at least fifteen people wide that reached down the avenue as far as we could see. A sudden bang – the official starting gun – elicited a round of excited applause and some whoops. And then we stood for another five minutes, hopping from one leg to another and shuffling along, bit by bit, as stern-looking people around us checked water bottles, food supplies, headphones and playlists. And then there was the start point and the big red digital clock.

I don't remember much of the first 3 miles. We were moving, running, looking at each other occasionally, raising eyebrows and smiling and not thinking much. The first part of the route took us out of the path and down along the side of the river, towards Temple. It wasn't very nice – a long, straight road past bands of runners already coming back up the other side. I was starting to feel uncomfortable and realised I'd put on far too many clothes. Karen and I kept pace, watching what those around us were doing. To my immediate right, an odd character loped along, wearing 1970s' Dunlop 'bumpers' as my dad would call them – long, flat white trainers that he flopped down hard with every huge stride he took. Every ten or so strides, he would stop and walk, wiping sweat from his face. Then he'd start up again, flailing and thumping along. To Karen's left was a wheezy breather: a man in a pale blue T-shirt with a complexion of similar colour, who looked to be in extreme discomfort after 3.5 miles.

At this point I decided I wasn't going to last the whole run if I didn't take off some layers as I was starting to feel horribly hot. Glancing about, I saw that although the runners were still bunched tightly there were few spectators along this less picturesque part of the route. Quickly, and still running, I peeled off my vest, emblazoned with the National Autistic Society logo, and then took off the surplus T-shirt I was wearing beneath it. I happened to look up and realised there were about three hundred people watching from a bridge above as I ran along in my bra. Karen laughed and handed me back my vest as we ran beneath the bridge to cheers and whoops from the spectators.

Around 5 miles, Karen got a stitch and slowed. I stayed just ahead of her as we moved through Theatreland and turned left at Trafalgar Square, glancing back regularly to check her progress. 'Go ahead,' she mouthed, waving me on.

And then we were back into the park, streaming around the front of Buckingham Palace and down along a packed road of runners and spectators, flags flying, drums thrumming, cheers and whistles urging us along. I knew my family and the NAS crew were waiting at 7 miles and ran craning my head to see them. Suddenly to my left there was my sister, anxiously scanning the crowd. I jumped and waved and ran to her; she spotted me, and her face immediately lit up and then contorted into tears as a rush of emotion hit her. My mum and dad and little sister and baby niece all yelled my name and jumped up and down with glee. Delighted and thrilled, I moved up a gear and rocketed past them, grinning, to where my husband stood with the kids and the NAS staff, all waving madly and cheering. Moving faster now, I could see my husband and the boys and Betty and there, there was Grace – her sweet, sweet face and her hair blowing in the breeze – looking happy and anxious and pleased all at once. A huge sob escaped me. I blew kiss after kiss at her as I ran past. How could I have thought I was alone?

And then I had wings. From miles seven till ten I was absolutely flying: totally wired and excited and fuelled by a massive adrenaline rush. I could do this. And more: I was loving it. I overtook people, motored through the bends and handled several inclines with ease. I caught up with the pace-setter, bearing the flag for two hours ten minutes and passed him. It was beyond wonderful. My legs were like pistons. I felt sure and strong and absolutely invincible. The hair on the back of my neck tingled with the pleasure and excitement of it. At 10 miles I saw my husband and kids again, calling and clapping. Grace had her arms out over the barrier, reaching to me. 'Mummy!' she shouted. 'My mummy!'

At this point I thought: we look comfortable. I'm running with a pack of proper runners, and we're easing along. Then I noticed the people on the other side of the barrier, pushing back up the hill. These people were ahead of us. Some of them did not look comfortable. Some of them did not look well at all.

We surged downhill and turned – it was 10.5 miles along and, abruptly, I did not feel like an Olympian any more. My legs felt thick and my feet were landing heavily. I was starting to feel a bit sick. At mile eleven, I was suppressing extreme discomfort and the first whisper of panic. At mile twelve I remembered that the race was not 13 miles at all, but 13.1 miles. That 0.1 of a mile was a game-changer. I couldn't possibly run more than 13 miles. I would never do it. People were passing me now on either side: people who had kept something in reserve. They were checking their watches, nodding with satisfaction, going up a gear. Neat ponytails bobbed in front of me. Straight-backed muscle men went into fifth gear and whooshed past. I let loose a torrent of obscenities under my breath. I'd done this all wrong. My run was more of a stagger by now. Beside me another runner slowed to a walk, shaking her head with regret.

I told myself: I will not walk. I will *not*.

Ahead of me was a sign announcing that there were 800 metres to go. It might as well have said another 8 miles. By now, I was weaving with exhaustion.

Then came a sign saying 400 metres, and I thought: maybe.

Then came a sign saying 200 metres, and I could see the finishing line. I experimented, asking my legs to move faster. They did. I asked them to go faster still. They did. I straightened my shoulders. I was running, properly running again. The crowds of spectators on either side of me were three deep and roaring approval. A massive grin split my face. I was purely, blissfully happy.

As I went over the finish line, my body suddenly spasmed with sobs. Around me people bent over and grabbed their knees, or clutched each other in ecstasy, or shook hands and blew out hard. The first person I recognised in the crowd was my sister. I made my way to her on legs made of water and she held me fast while I cried. 'My sister,' she said. 'Oh, my sister.' We were both crying and laughing. My mum was there and hugged me. My dad appeared, so moved he could hardly talk. My little sister hugged me so tightly that what little puff I had left was expelled and I had to ask her weakly to let go now.

For a while, my parents and sisters and I stood by our arranged meeting point, going over and over the scene, laughing and remarking on details and people and how marvellous everything was. I had caught my breath and was starting to realise that I had finished a half-marathon. Around my neck was the carved wooden medallion of the

Royal Parks Society. Other runners walking past with friends and family nodded at me, smiling. I was part of a community now. I could stand tall. I had come such a long way, in all senses. But I couldn't relax.

And then I saw them, before they saw me. My family. A stumbling raggle-taggle herded by a single adult on the verge of extreme exasperation. Grace was scanning the crowds and crying with frustration at being unable to find me in the numbers of people. Betty was wearing a National Autistic Society T-shirt the same size as her and looked bored. The boys looked weary. My husband looked weary. (Later they told me that the wheel had come off Betty's buggy and they had had to struggle with it across miles of mushy park grass from the 10-mile marker to get to the finishing point.) But then they saw me and wiped their expressions clean of everything but love and pride; they rushed to me and I was enveloped in hugs and kisses and congratulations.

From the tangle of arms and heads, Grace's face emerged. She gazed up at me. I gazed back at her: my daughter, my first-born, the grace of my heart named for the gift that she was to me. Her beautiful eyes, her nose, her precious, clever mouth. I could feel her arms wrapped around my waist as she squeezed me. I freed one of my own arms and pushed her hair back from her face. The hubbub around us faded. Grace glinted at me with an expression of pride and gratitude and love. I will remember that look for the rest of my life.

Part Three

I spent the first days after the race in a teary, exhausted haze. I wanted to talk about it constantly and relive every moment. Then I would want silence and solitude to rest and consider. As in the days immediately after childbirth, I was worn out and exhilarated and bruised and hyper. A laugh would end in tears. A groaning shuffle to the sofa would transform halfway into a waltz and a whoop.

My husband was very patient.

I had a sense that everything had changed. I was giddy with the promise and potential of what I had found: a role in which I could make money – in the old-fashioned way, by sweaty toil – to be spent on improving life for people with autism and Asperger's Syndrome. By running the Royal Parks, I'd collected some £1200 which, with a charitable donation from my workplace, was likely to reach £1800. When I told the staff at the National Autistic Society I could feel my voice tremble with the pleasure and passion of it. I had done a good, good thing.

I posted pictures of myself everywhere: captured in a snapshot on the finishing line looking pink and flushed and ecstatic in my NAS running vest. I debated on Twitter whether my finishing time was honourable or not. I wrote Facebook captions full of exclamation marks about how wonderful it had been. I emailed friends and family, ostensibly to say thank you, and to point out again how much I had raised and how hard I had worked. And, of course, I blogged about it.

I was high on my own success.

Meanwhile, Grace continued to go to school every day. She seemed calm. She was drawing a lot and her mania for Monster High seemed as strong as ever. Most of her sentences started with a description of a new character she had invented, or a dream that she'd had about them, or a play that she'd written about them. But there were long, lucid enough periods in between. And our scuffles over homework were muted.

Then one evening when I was putting her light out and tucking her in to bed, she started to talk in torrents. A girl at school – whose behaviour had been making me quietly uneasy since the start of term – had gone for her. Following weeks of spiteful asides and snidely determined whispers engineered to undermine Grace, this child had fronted her out in the playground and told her to stop making claims on any of her friends. They were, she proclaimed with relish, only being nice to her because she had Asperger's Syndrome.

With her hands over her face, weeping and rocking under her duvet, Grace recounted to me her reaction. Spinning with dismay she had shouted back. And, bless them, several of her friends had stoutly defended her. Later, with the conscientiousness of nine-year-olds, they recounted in detail to Grace everything that this other child had been saying about her over the weeks, all of it pure poison.

Any parent will know the sick, dark feeling that spreads like an ink stain over your heart when your child tells you they are in pain. Mine was extra bitter, compounded by shame and remorse. All the while I had been congratulating myself on changing the world, Grace was trudging through a parallel universe where everything was just the same.

I talked to the school. I watched that child like a hawk. And I started listening to my daughter again.

And after some time off, I began running again. This time for the London Marathon, hoping that some of the millions of people watching the event – in a year when more tourists than usual were flocking to the city to watch the Olympics – would see the name of the charity written on my chest and would want to know more and want to help.

I remembered who and what I was running for.

11

The Surrealist Manifesto

If someone had sat me down at that point and explained to me the process I would have to endure in order to finally and conclusively get Grace the help she needed at school, I would not have believed them.

By this point, as Grace entered Year 5, she had a weary boxer's attitude to school: eventually, she reasoned, someone would tell her it was over and possibly present her with whatever it was she'd been fighting for, even if it was only the runners-up prize. In the meantime, she had learned to adopt a primarily defensive stance and, head down, abandon any attempts to demonstrate skill or initiative in a bid to just survive. I desperately wanted to get her out of the school, but I couldn't afford to stop work and home-school her, and she refused point blank to countenance the idea of starting again somewhere else.

Our request for help from the local authority had been turned down in Year 4, the previous year. After we got Grace's formal diagnosis, the school had asked for extra resources, only to be told that we had not sufficiently proved our case. I was aggrieved and disappointed and angry. As the new term got under way and we prepared to try again, it became clear to me that I still had a lot to learn about what this application entailed.

I had thought the school had it covered. I was wrong. They were almost as much in the dark as I was. They had applied for and secured help for other children, but demonstrating the needs of a child with Aspergers – that curious twilight between 'normal' and 'disabled' – seemed to flummox them. The onus, it felt, was on me.

Often I imagine telling someone else what it's like, this operation. It's only ever an imagining because detailing it all would be almost as exhausting as actually doing it. And I can't believe that anyone would really want to listen for long.

I think the conversation would go a little like this:

Right now, concentrate. Put that down, whatever it is and pay attention. You need a what? It's all right, I'll wait. Perhaps a cup of tea would be nice, yes.

OK, so you're ready. Yes, I'm still here. Now, I'm going to tell you about something called a statement of educational needs and what it's like trying to get one. No, come back. No really, you do need to know this. It tells you everything about the way the government sees your child. And it tells you a lot about the pain and required patience of parenting a child that doesn't quite fit in.

Sorry. Yes, all right, I'll drop the martyred tone. (I'll try, anyway.) No, I didn't say anything then. Just clearing my throat. Ahem.

So. Imagine your child is not keeping up in class. If you're lucky, her teacher will a) notice and b) care. Often if parts a) and b) are met, then your child may be put on something called School Action, or School Action Plus. (I don't know why we use the words 'put on' – they're not drugs – but we do.) These terms mean that your child will receive a number of hours' help a week, usually on a one-to-one basis, with the aim of helping them catch up in the areas where they need support.

If after this has happened your child is still struggling and/or in distress, then the school may suggest talking to an educational psychologist. (Unless your child only admits problems once he or she gets home, in which case the school will tell you there's nothing wrong, regardless of any further incidents, tra-la-la fingers in our ears, we can't hear you.)

At some point, the educational psychologist will look at your child and may then decide that there's an underlying diagnosis to be made which will enable everyone to get the correct help for your child. You're told this will be the next step.

Now wait for a bit, probably several weeks. Or it could be months. No, I don't know why. No, I don't know precisely how long. Yes, you can ask. People will talk about 'resources' and put the phone down on you.

Eventually, you'll get a date for an assessment. With a clinical psychologist and a paediatrician and perhaps also a speech and language therapist and maybe an occupational health therapist too for good measure. It may be one or some or all of the above. It may take half an hour or it may take all morning. This will be a couple of months further on again. When you turn up for your assessment, you may also get the diagnosis then. It may happen that quickly because, by now, your child will be fairly upset or switched off entirely or generally disruptive. Let's pick a diagnosis – let's say autism. You may be told this on the day, or you may be told this a while afterwards on the phone. You might get a letter. Or you could wait for a few more weeks and make a few more phone calls before someone will tell you.

OK, so now your child has a label. Congratulations. You've now been set apart from the mainstream, and if your child goes to an academy or any school which prides itself on results and academic prowess, you may find that it is suggested you leave and go somewhere else more appropriate. Or you might just find that the school doesn't know what autism is and ignores the diagnosis. Or you might find that the school does want to help, but doesn't have the resources to do so. They will start talking about something called a statement. If you're in this last category, congratulations. You have won the Golden Ticket. Really. You have. But you're a long, long way off from claiming any prizes.

At this point, it's probably at least a year since you first had that conversation with your kid's teacher about something being not quite right. It may be several years since you had that first conversation with your kid's nursery teacher about something being not quite right. Feeling a bit uneasy and anxious? Get used to it. Camomile or mint tea are quite calming. So is running massively long distances. Or you could just open a bottle of wine. But be careful. You've got to be able to concentrate in the morning. You've got to be able to concentrate all the time in fact. You can't ever, ever not concentrate. Ever again.

So now you and your school have to ask for extra help from the local authority to get this thing called a statement of educational needs, which is basically like bestowing a bursary on your child, to be spent by whichever school they are at on whatever help they need. Take a deep breath. It's about to get even more complicated. (Unless you're loaded and can just pay for a classroom assistant to be with your child all day, and give private tuition in the subjects they don't understand; in which case, hand over the cheque and everything is sorted. No, didn't think you could.) OK, so now you are in a process in which you ask for a statutory assessment.

There can't be something good on the telly, it's four-thirty in the afternoon. I promise I won't take much longer.

A statutory assessment is an investigation carried out by the local authority to find out what your child's special educational needs are and what provision is needed to meet those needs.

This is where you have to pay close attention. Are you listening? In order to request a statutory assessment to find out what your child's special educational needs are and what provision is needed to meet those needs, *you* have to first find out yourself what your child's special educational needs are, and ask loads of experts precisely what support your child should be getting – like one-to-one help in the class-room, an assistant to sit with them and take them through the subjects they don't understand, social-skills classes and practical interventions in the playground, occupational therapy, sensory assessments and alterations to the physical conditions in the classroom – and then ask loads of teach-ers to try to provide it. This will take about another year. Only when you have detailed precisely what your child's needs are, what resources your child needs and have bullied/coerced/begged the school's teachers and special educational needs co-ordinators to provide as much of that specialised teaching as is possible, can you then apply to the council to please establish what your child's special educa-tional needs are and what provision is needed to meet those needs.

There is a special trick to this application. Get it right, and the council will agree to a statutory assessment of your child. Get it wrong, and they will throw out all of your paperwork and assessments and requests on the grounds that you haven't proved your point. I think (but I'm not sure) that you have to show there's a problem that you've tried to fix, but that you can't quite do it. Woe betide you if you haven't tried hard enough – or if you have tried too hard, and look like you may be doing OK on your own.

Anyway, no one quite knows what this special trick is. Where I live, educational experts give workshops to parents on how to apply for a statutory assessment. They are not allowed to give them to teachers or special educational needs co-ordinators in schools. I have no idea why, but I suspect it's to make sure we don't all get together and figure it out. There's not a lot of money in that pot for extra help: they can't have hordes of people coming at them with watertight cases. So you have to really focus intently on all the worst aspects of your child, all the most negative, upsetting, miserable experiences and difficulties they have. It's a bonus if you can get a doctor or two to say formally just how very fucked up they are. Never mind if it makes you feel sad. Just do it.

So now you've sent off your letter. By now your child may well have just given up on school. He or she may be being bullied because they are so clearly separate from the rest of the class. He or she might not be sleeping. Perhaps he or she is having panic attacks. Excitement about new ideas and learning will have gone entirely out of the window.

If you're very very very very lucky and you discovered what that special trick was, you will be told six weeks later that the local authority thinks you have made a good enough case to assess your child and see if/whether/what kind of special help they need.

So then the local authority will begin its own process of evaluating your child and his or her needs. It will do this by asking all the same people that you asked to assess your child again. It will ask all those people to write the same reports that they already have. And it might ask for a few more, just in case.

This process can take a month, or it can take six months.

At the end of it, they can say no.

When that happens, you have a right to appeal.

How much do you know about the legal system in this country?

No, come back ...

Two months into the new term I was starting to become aware of the awfulness of the system in which I was now irrevocably trapped, at least until we had an outcome of some sort. Asking around friends and other parents whether they knew this feeling, several concurred.

'It's horrendous. It is the worst thing ever. It is awful. It is emotionally draining,' said Kelly of her fight for Jack. 'My advice is: prepare yourself for a long fight, and a long wait. It's not going to be easy.'

The local education authority had instructed us, on rejecting our first application the previous year, to make more use of the resources available in the borough before asking for more money. At this point Grace had been seen, over the course of six years since that first lifted eyebrow from her nursery school teacher, by three GPs, three paediatricians, one educational psychologist, one clinical psychologist and three speech therapists, from a variety of countries and London boroughs, marking our recent peregrinations. We had submitted reports from all of them, at least three of which strongly recommended that Grace would benefit from a statement of educational needs.

Regardless, our request was rejected on the grounds that we hadn't done enough research. We were told to go away and ask our local borough's own team for their take on Grace and their suggestions on how we could help her.

This experience is far from unusual, said Chris, father to four-and-a-half-year-old Ethan, who is diagnosed as high-functioning autistic.

'We had the educational psychologist see Ethan three times and provide a detailed report about why he needed a state-ment: he needs direction all the time or he closes down,' he told me. 'We had the statement from his nursery and one from the consultant who saw him first. But the verdict was clearly reached in five minutes by an apparatchik in a coun-cil who had never clapped eyes on our son and took a decision based on resources – though they deny it.'

Nathan's mum Sam added: 'The system is fundamentally flawed. It is designed to confuse; you are given as little infor-mation as possible. Just reading the information about the process is baffling. A lot of my friends got knocked down at the first hurdle.'

So, duly knocked back, the school and I did as we had been told and made a list of the people we needed to call. We started making appointments – badgering people with already massive caseloads to find time to see one more child, to confirm what ten other people had already told us. One by one, they came in to see Grace and, slowly, the new stacks of paperwork that would make the case for our next attempt started to mount. But it took so very, very long. And the rec-ommendations were not enough – we had to understand them and try to implement them. The school had other chil-dren to get on and teach, and the special needs co-ordinator often looked as harassed as I at the latest report. I felt as though I was constantly rushing between the experts and the school, nipping and barking at them like a sheepdog to get them moving – oh so slowly – in the right direction. And all while trying to work and look after my toddler and run the household. And just run, which felt more and more like bolting away from it all each time I stepped over the threshold and shut the front door behind me.

'How much time did it take to get the help we need? Well, my wife gave up work,' said Chris. 'It involves a lot of chasing. You chase the speech and language people, you chase up the physical therapy appointments. You have to keep monitoring the social side to make sure that his behaviour is socially appropriate. Our local authority is swamped. We were assigned a case worker, but we rarely hear from her because she's so busy.'

So this is how I now spend my time.

Today, at work, I sat in a shuttered meeting room in front of a neat line of empty chairs and a tripod-shaped phone that squatted on a polished table like a robotic claw. I took off my watch and regarded it, aware of my empty desk elsewhere in the building, an abandoned chair and an impatient flashing cursor at the top of a blank screen. I decided I had ten minutes to complete the task I had set myself before what could pass for a wee-and-a-cup-of-tea break started to look suspiciously more like a dereliction of duties.

On the table in front of me was another report bearing my daughter's name, the stamp of the local borough and a long list of names of those who had been sent copies. The report was seven pages long and it said that on top of the recommendations of the last two reports (to whit: assess my daughter for dyscalculia; call in the local authority's anti-bullying sub group; provide a safe room to which she can go when she needs to; give her extra time for tasks but keep subjects to a fifteen-minute limit; review class social dynamics and underscore positive peer reactions to her), we should also now refer her to occupational therapy to look at sensory issues and how they might be affecting her work and behaviour. The woman who wrote the report suggested that certain hypersensitivity to touch and noise was at play in Grace's underperformance and disruptive behaviour, and also some hyposensitivity. I didn't know what that meant.

On another page, the assessor had written: 'There may also be issues with her vestibular and proprioceptive senses.'

I didn't know what that meant, either.

I scanned the front page of the report again. The author's name was written there, and her title. There was no contact number, no address. I rifled quickly through the pages again. There was no contact number anywhere.

So I started by telephoning the council switchboard (using my personal mobile phone, not the claw) and asked to speak to the author of the report.

'We haven't got anyone of that name listed.'

'She's written a report about my daughter . . .'

'Putting you through to Children's Services.'

A pause.

'Hello, Children's Services.'

'Hello, I'd like to speak to [name].'

'I don't know her. Hold on, I'll look her up.'

'I think she's on the advisory team.'

Pause.

'I've found a number for her – here it is –'

'Could you put me through, please?'

'Could I? Oh. [Doubtful] Er. Hang on.'

Pause. Click.

New voice: 'Hello?'

'Hello, are you [name]? I've got your report about my daughter.'

'No, I'm sorry. I'm not her.'

'Ah. I was put through to you by Children's Services.'

'Sorry. What's the name of the person you want? I'll look her up.'

'[Name.]'

'Here she is. Ah, no, that's my number. They've put my number here. That's why you can't find her.'

'Right. She works for the advisory team. Do you know that number?'

'I can look up someone else on that team. Perhaps they can help. Maybe she's left or something.'

'Ah. OK. Thanks.'

Pause. Click.

New voice: 'Hello?'

'Hello, I'm looking for [name].'

'Hang on.'

Muffled discussion in the background. I heard the name of the woman I was seeking being said by several voices in varying questioning tones. Then one exclaimed: 'Oh!' and pronounced the name in recognition. My shoulders sagged with relief.

The voice came back to the phone: 'She's not based here. I'll have a look on the system.'

I waited in silence, the minutes passing.

'Are you there? She's at [name of] school. Call this number.'

I hung up. Eight minutes had passed. I dialled again.

New voice: 'Hello?'

'Hello? I'm looking for [name]. She's written a report about my daughter, but I can't seem to find her.'

'Can't you? Awww. She's here. Hang on.'

I waited in silence and as I waited I thought of Grace's face looking out of the car window in profile against the amber dusk as we drove home last night. I thought of her saying blankly, apropos of nothing: 'I don't deserve my friends, Mummy. Because I get all cross and I lose my temper at them and shout. And they're just nice.'

When the new voice came on and said: 'Hello?' I breathed in and forced a friendly, all-the-time-in-the-world, polite tone into my voice and said:

'Hello? [Name]? I've got your report about my daughter and I wondered whether you might have a few minutes for a chat. I've got some questions, you see ... '

And so it continued – the hassle and pushing – until a couple of weeks later, I got in from work and staggered upstairs to finally pause and reflect on my day, which had been thoroughly rotten but also revelatory.

Beneath the purple velvet throw, a shape on my bed squirmed and stifled giggles. Betty was hiding under the covers. Grace, who had entered behind me, and I glanced at each other and nodded conspiratorially, smiling. With a whoop, we dashed to reveal her, but at just that moment my two-year-old daughter flung back the covers and sat bolt upright, hair a perfect dandelion of static, shouting and pointing at us: 'Found oo!'

We collapsed on our knees, protesting that that wasn't how the game went. Beaming and magnanimous, Betty beckoned us in. 'C'mon: hiding,' she said to Grace and me. We got into bed on either side of her and she pulled the coverlet over our heads.

In the dark, everyone's giggles subsided. In the silence I could hear the slow breathing of my big girl and the rhythmic wet tug of Betty sucking her fingers. I could smell the top of Betty's head and the sweetness of her breath. Grace's hand curled around to find mine and I kissed her slender fingers, stroking a rough patch over one knuckle.

Cocooned and peaceful for the first time in ages, I thought about what had happened that day.

It started as I travelled to work pre-dawn, surrounded by grey commuters, watching warped reflections in the curved train window and fretting about the state of my bank account. As I sat, stiffly working through the same sums in my head and failing repeatedly to find a bigger total, my co-travellers shook out newspapers and gravely consumed articles about economic crisis, spiralling debt, political unrest. I thought about my below-inflation pay rise (make that sub-zero, below-inflation pay rise) and the contrasting mountainous peaks of our household outgoings. Beside me, a young man read a book called *Think and Grow Rich*, underlining in blue pen passages about using the subconscious to bring lucrative ideas to fruition. His fingernails were bitten to the quick. The time was six-thirty in the morning. The carriage smelled of recession.

Work was better, enlivened by lovely colleagues and appreciation of what I did and the kind of black-humoured desk banter that supports and salves and acknowledges the really gloomy stuff only by poking fun at it.

But then as ever, there were the bloody phone calls, the same tedious, depressing phone calls. The latest meeting, the latest conversation about the latest report, the latest tiny, tiny suggestion of a baby step towards progress. Redoing the numbers in my head again and wondering about paying for extra help, if it might help Grace faster. Redoing my work shifts in my head again and wondering how to ask for the next bit of time off for the next appointment, or presentation for parents, or training that I dared not miss as I attempted to garner information and points. Fretting about time, fretting about money, fretting about how long this could possibly last without a resolution.

'Any initial relief I had on finally getting Harry diagnosed was replaced by financial worries,' Amanda said to me when I asked her if she fretted this way. 'Any parent of a child with special needs whether mild or severe will inevitably find that they have a much higher expenditure than other parents. I have paid privately for cognitive behavioural therapy because the NHS waiting list was eighteen months and he needed the treatment sooner. In the future, I wonder, will I have to support him financially, emotionally, practically for longer than my other children? For as long as I am able?'

Casting my mind forward into an impossibly black future,

I wound myself ever more tightly. And then someone told me to belt up.

Have you ever asked for help, wailed about being stressed, gone on and on and on about the injustice and the fatigue of it, got angrier and angrier and then been told: 'Oh, belt up'?

Neither had I.

Boy, was it liberating.

Because actually, I realised, this one overloaded, irritated person had given voice to what everyone else had been saying all along. Translated, the government had long been telling me to belt up, to tighten my belt, to cut back, to manage. The local authority had long been telling me to belt up, to go away, to take my complaints and my needy daughter and just put a sock in it. The school had said to me belt up, we know, we're working on it, we can't perform miracles. In the business world in which I worked, the current mantra was: look, it's rough out there, we like you, it's time for everyone to make sacrifices: now take this and belt up.

It's just that so far, everyone had been a bit more polite about it than that and I, sap that I was, had responded to their bland words by wrinkling my nose and making vague noises of displeasure and shuffling away to groan quietly to myself. Faced now with a direct insult, I passed quickly through shock, then outrage, then anger so pure I thought I might have a heart attack.

And then: I saw the world for what it really was and the true nature of the abuse that had been coming my way for a while now. It wasn't personal. It just was what it was. I could laugh and shake my head and counter with the knowledge that I had a secret weapon that would see me through.

So that evening I lay on the bed with Grace and Betty and thought: when the girls are asleep and my husband is back from work, I will go running. Quickly, before I can change my mind, I will change into my thermal long-sleeved top, my running tights, my shorts; I will don jumper and hat and socks. Outside it will be black and cold and squally with rain. I will wince and angle my head to avoid the worst of it and I will run and run and run and sometimes, when the traffic is loud, I will shout rude words and roar like a madwoman and no one will hear me.

But, I told myself, I will not be silenced and I will finish this marathon.

This drive, this insistence on being heard, is an essential component of being a parent of a child with autism, judging by what other mothers and father have told me.

'If you're not outspoken, you'll fall at the first hurdle,' Nathan's mum Sam said. 'It's a system and you have to play the system. Keep the local authority on your side, but never take any of their advice at face value – you have to remember that many of the workers you talk to are employed by the body who wants to keep the numbers of statements down. It's not you who are paying their wages.'

To make a convincing case, Sam advised me to write everything down. 'Record every incident that your child has, every bad day, so you can paint as full a picture as possible,' she said.

So I did. While the school compiled its case, I

constructed the parental statement that would support that request. I jotted down all the tears and hysteria and misery. Doing so made me feel hysterical and off-balance, disloyal to my daughter and as though I was deliberately overlooking the parts of her that evened her out into the marvellous individual before me. It was soul-destroying. But I had to do it.

And gradually, gradually, the tentative equilibrium that I had established since the darkest days of the year before started to see-saw. That constant feeling of uneasy sickness returned. Getting up in the mornings felt like preparing for battle. I stopped laughing or making jokes, entirely unable to join in family banter. One day my husband looked closely at my face and said: 'Let's go away for a few days.'

We left Grace and her stepbrothers with their other parents, our former partners, and ran away, mid-week, mid-November, mid-term. We stayed on an island on the Atlantic coast in a tiny, exquisite jewel of a house that belonged to a friend of my husband. It was decorated in shades of mushroom and oyster and duck-egg blue. The brass-framed beds were heaped with ivory quilts and white lace cushions. A row of dearly dented copper pans twinkled in the postage-stamp-sized kitchen. On one wall hung a limited edition black and white photograph of a very young Brigitte Bardot, all hair and mouth. Betty stood in front of it and pointed and said: 'Grace.'

With my husband, I went for a walk along a coastal path, holding Betty, who pressed her face to mine, imparting sticky, snotty kisses while with both hands clutching at the wind in her hair. A seagull flew low overhead and we looked up and she laughed to see its downy belly and yellow feet. I felt her arms around my neck and her feet in little boots kicking my hips while I folded my arms under her bottom. Her tiny white sharp teeth and rosy tongue were those of a little animal. I was swoony with adoration for her and I felt a sudden terrible pang for Grace.

That night, in the bedroom we were all sharing, I listened to Betty chatter in her sleep: alternately sunny and stern and anxious. I got up four times to stroke her cheek and smooth her hair when her murmurings took on a more plaintive tone. When I got up the next morning, I drank two mugs of hot bitter coffee, so strong that it left a dry residue on my teeth. Then I went for a run. I had to do 7 miles: marathon training kicked in for real in two weeks and I had to keep up a basic level of fitness. My eyes looked like poached eggs and my gait was shambolic after five minutes. My husband pedalled alongside me on a rented bicycle with Betty grinning from the back seat beneath a helmet that made her look like a mushroom.

It was a glorious morning. The sun was bright and the dark blue sea fluttered and glittered to my right as I crunched along the white gravel path. The air was sharp with the tang of seaweed and oyster beds. We passed bushes of grey-green foliage. It was almost not credible that we were six weeks from Christmas. I was sweating in my running top and struggling for air. I forced myself to run straighter, more upright. I clenched my stomach muscles and moved my arms like pistons. At elbow height, Betty continued to smile cheerily at me. I pushed away thoughts of how on earth I would keep this up for 26 miles and tried to live in the present.

London – dark, cold, rainy, with the hole in our bedroom window and our condemned boiler and my file spilling out reports on Grace – seemed a lifetime away. We were flat broke, but we had broken into our savings and bought budget airline tickets to get here. I felt worried and guilty thinking about the money we had spent, that we could scarcely afford, to get away from the lifestyle that we could scarcely keep up. I thought of the cost of Grace's birthday party in three weeks' time. I thought of Grace. I had left the coast road and was running past white-walled streets and out across long flat vineyards where orange leaves trembled on the breeze. My husband called out exclamations of enjoyment at the day, at the scenery, at the buildings and landscape. We passed a cluster of old men pointing giant, ancient shotguns into a copse where unfortunate fowl were hiding. A little later, we passed a church where Mass was just ending and the last strains of plainsong encircled us.

There was no television in the house and no phone or internet reception. That evening we listened to music and drank wine and watched candles flicker on the exposed sandstone bricks of the sitting room. I felt very happy and very in love and I could not shake the guilt of being there without Grace, instead of being in London to pick her up from school and ask questions about her day with a casualness that belied an intense anxiety and a mental checklist of how she did in lessons, in the playground, at lunchtime, now. My husband listened patiently while I stuttered to him how I was feeling.

Gently, he tried to tell me in a nice way that it wasn't all about me, actually. That I was doing what I could and that I could only do that and that she was getting on fine and that she was with her dad and things were progressing and that I should give myself a break.

But still, the guilt insinuated itself into my enjoyment of the enchanting place.

The next day Betty was in a grotty mood when she woke from her afternoon nap. She played with her dollies on the sofa, trying to cover them up and tuck them in with a blanket that was far too big. Her movements were jerky with impatience and she was muttering under her breath. I listened in and realised she was saying 'fuck*sake*' in exactly my tones. I was mortified and guilty all over again. Is this what I am? A muttering, cursing grouch? I reddened with shame while my husband stifled laughter. Ridiculously, the guilt had become yet another thing to feel worried and resentful – and guilty – about. I had to find a way to break free of it.

We went for a drive as the sun was setting, our little rental Renault belting along narrow roads the length of the island. Suddenly we left a cluster of buildings and shot out into miles and miles of salt flats silently reflecting the damson twilight. The land seemed vast and endless; the skies stretched above and around and they were all there was. I felt tiny and insignificant. Finally, I could breathe.

I came back to London full of vigour for the task ahead. The appointments for Grace kept coming round, the latest experts eyed her over, the paperwork piled up higher: slowly, gradually, we were making our case. I went to see Grace's teacher once a week for progress checks and to swap ideas on how to help Grace. I emailed the headteacher and the special educational needs co-ordinator (the SENCo) regularly to see how much progress they were making and called meetings every six weeks to run through which reports had arrived and which were still to be chased up, how the teacher's timesheets and observations were coming along, whether we had updated Grace's latest individual education plan to show how little she had advanced since the start of term. It felt like drawing a pointillist picture of my daughter in black and grey and bilious yellow.

There were constant hiccups and delays.

At one meeting, I turned up having emailed everyone a four-page agenda and summary. They had all only printed three pages and had not read the summary. We proceeded with the meeting anyway – it was so hard to find a time when everyone was free – and I fought to keep my temper every time I raised a point that was on page four, and received blank looks.

A few weeks later, the SENCo toiled through an assessment for dyscalculia with Grace and I revised my opinion of her. Doggedly, she educated herself in this excruciating process and completed it, while the local authority expert who had recommended it be done stopped answering emails requesting her input. I sat down and wrote my final statement, explaining my worries for Grace as her mother and how her upset and difficulties at school were spilling into our home life. Grace wrote a letter in which she explained how miserable school was making her.

I kept telling myself: this is necessary. It will make things better for her.

Then eventually, several weeks later, I stood in the reception of my local council offices one morning waiting to deliver a large brown envelope packed with evidence that my daughter needed help.

It had snowed overnight, and as I waited there, the thick entrance doors sliced open and closed with a slushy mechanical wheeze, conveying blinking, wet-faced employees into the building, along with runnels of stained water that made patterns in the cheap carpet underfoot.

I looked at the succession of people passing me, shaking their hair and the snow from their boots, and wondered if any of them would be making the decision about Grace's future: the decision that would make an entirely different life for her. I had asked the receptionist to see Grace's case worker and been told that he was not at his desk, but that a message would be left for him to come down as soon as he appeared, which would be shortly.

I was about to hand over a mountain of deeply personal reports and assessments which, in clinical tones, told of my daughter's mind and heart and self, to a man I had never before met, who would then take them away, show them to a panel of more people I had never met and would not know, then write to me a few weeks later to tell me whether or not this group of anonymous deciders had been sufficiently moved to grant our request for additional support.

A yes would mean the money for an assistant to work one-to-one with her in the classroom and to help her navigate the social minefield of the playground. It would open the door to the best secondary school in the area, with its team of support workers and autism-friendly teaching methods and its drama and art studios where Grace could thrive and bloom.

A no would mean the dull continuation of daily struggle and bullying and constant barely suppressed terror at what life at the local comprehensive would entail. A no would mean a long, long legal battle to change the local authority's verdict. A no would mean living even deeper in debt as we scrambled to pull together enough money to pay for some help ourselves.

So I wanted to see this man – the only face in the chain that I was indeed likely to be allowed to see. We had spoken on the phone a couple of times; most recently two weeks earlier when I had rung to say that the school and I were working together on preparing our second application attempt and to ask if I could bring it to him in person to meet him on this date. He had agreed.

I looked at the clock on the wall. It showed me that ten minutes had passed since my arrival. I sat down on a hard felt sofa and removed my hat. My stomach was knotted and my hands tingled slightly with nerves. I smoothed the surface of the envelope, feeling its hard bulk under my fingers, and hoped for the hundredth time that we'd got it right, that we'd done enough. In the last few weeks, I had called upon everyone I thought might be useful to seek advice on the final presentation. To the obvious dismay of the SENCo, exhausted from weeks of typing and collating material, I had asked her just the previous morning to rewrite sections of it along the lines suggested by some of the experts I had asked to comment on the draft. Ignoring my discomfort, I had also at the same meeting edited the headteacher's letter and asked for some other changes to be made. As late as the previous evening, I was still emailing and calling the school to check the final version. When I picked up the final package for delivery, I mentally congratulated the staff on still being able to raise a smile when they saw me. I pushed away the memory from the previous week when I discovered their copy of the code of practice – the special educational needs bible for schools – was dated 1994.

More council staff walked past me, the laggards now, tugging off scarves and checking their BlackBerrys as they passed. I dug my phone out of my pocket and checked the time. Seventeen minutes had passed.

At that moment, a tired-looking woman in a smart skirt and jumper approached me and asked if I was waiting for X. I said I was. She told me that he was very busy and had sent her to collect my package, rather than coming down himself.

Numbly I handed it over and watched her take it from me. She turned to go and in a rush I said: 'I really hope it works.' The woman looked slightly embarrassed and nodded.

Then I put my hat on and walked back out into the snow, so bright it made my eyes sting.

12

What have I got myself into?

Meanwhile, somehow, amid the din of everything, I was by now doing some serious running. Marathon training had kicked in, there were fewer than sixteen weeks to go until London 2012, and despite all the miles that had I had completed since that first wheezy tour of the local swings, I was only now beginning to register the scale of the challenge I had set myself.

Marathon training. How had I missed the clue in the name?

When I decided to run the London Marathon I hadn't given much thought to the process of preparation. Sure, I thought it would be pretty hard: you don't just get out of bed one day and run 26 miles without some kind of limbering-up process. (Well, you can, and people do; but they're usually the ones on a stretcher or on the ground somewhere around mile twelve.) Yet when it came to visualising that hardness – all the tears and sweat and blisters and mud – my mind was only really providing a cartoon version in which I staggered over the finish line looking glamorously dishevelled and triumphant. Despite every tough run and every sit-up I'd done to date, I still had no clue about what I'd got myself into, as the early days of serious marathon training would show me.

Way back in June when the idea first presented itself to me, I had asked my friend Kate – who has run the marathon in a time that makes grown men blanch – what the training involved and just how tough it would be. She laughed and said: 'You just run. And run. Then you keep running. And you eat lots of bananas.'

So I had started running. That was that box ticked.

Then somewhere in the early months – back in summer, those lovely days of sunlight that I took so much for granted – I had discovered that getting a marathon place wasn't as straightforward as I had expected. Naively, I had imagined some kind of scenario in which I would step forward proudly, perhaps slightly bashfully ('No, really, don't clap') and giving a gracious nod, announce my participation, upon which grateful organisers would deferentially usher me in, perhaps shaking my hand and patting my back.

In reality I had to put my name into a ballot, pay a fee – refundable, but only if I was too much of a miser to donate it to charity – and hope to beat the odds to be one of the lucky ones. Everyone I told regaled me with tales of people who had applied for years with no success.

I then discovered (it's all in the research, folks: aren't you glad I've done yours for you?) that if I wanted to run the marathon for the National Autistic Society, I needed to apply to them separately. So again I stepped up, filled in the form, and waited to hear trumpets. Thank you very much, they told me, we'll be making our decision in a couple of months and we'll get back to you.

After an anxious wait (was I doing all this running for nothing?) I learned that I had not won a marathon place via the ballot, but that the National Autistic Society had invited me to be one of their 'gold bond' runners. I had a place on their team and a £2012 fundraising target to hit.

And I had a new routine, thanks to my trainer Amelia, who advised me in her bright, no-messing tones that I had to get myself seriously buff now, as well as upping the distances, if my body was to withstand the strain I was about to place on it. Since the half-marathon I'd slacked off. I'd been running 5 or 6 miles, two or three times a week, at a relatively gentle pace, more with a focus on de-stressing than increasing my fitness. Now, as the year drew to a close, I had to increase my mileage, increase the number of days I trained and increase the effort I was putting in. I had to do interval training (walk, jog, run, sprint, over and over again) and hill sprints (find the nearest sharp incline and pelt up it, twenty times) and mile pace runs (complete a certain number of miles in a specific time, usually some way outside my comfort zone) and strength work involving agonising lunges and squats. And the worst: upside-down sit-ups called jack-knife squats, which involved lying on a giant ball and pulling it towards me with my core and my knees while balancing my upper body on my hands. I had to work out five days a week. I had to take this very, very seriously.

So I started. I thought I was prepared. But what no one had prepared me for was that marathon training is basically running in the dark. (Unless you don't work and can fit it in during the day, in which case you have it easy, my friend: go and look for running sympathy elsewhere.) The races are generally in spring and the training takes three to four months. This means getting out there from December or January. The shock to my system was immense.

There are several options for running in the dark. You can run in the dark in the morning, before work, when the streets are cold and silent. You can run in the dark in the evening, once work is over and the kids are fed and bathed and put to bed, when the streets are cold and silent and every window you pass frames an imagined scene of cosiness and languor. You can also pretend you're not running in the dark – there are a couple of options here. You can run on a treadmill with the light on, forcing wakeful cheer as you grind away on the spot in the spare room and outside the streets are cold and silent, apart from slightly hysterical marathon runners who are at least breathing fresh air and watching passing scenery rather than that unloved armchair and the clothes rack. Or you can run outside with your eyes shut. This one doesn't work.

The exception to running in the dark was the weekend, when I got to stride out under brighter skies (or grey skies, or rainy skies, or windy ones.) This was bliss, not least because running in daylight meant parks and woods were safe again and I could pace to the sound of leaves crunching or birds singing: even in inclement weather the drip of rain on trees and grass was infinitely preferable to the dreary patter of it on pavements. The downside of this was that it was my Long Run. (This is the only run that other runners want to know about: 'How far did you go for your Long Run?' 'Long Run this weekend? How did it go?') So after a while running in daylight seemed like less of a gift when it meant I had to keep going for 11, 12, 13 miles, in the knowledge that the weeks ahead would require me to complete distances of 18, 19, 20 miles. I would have to set aside three hours or more and take a packed lunch.

But here's the thing. It was very, very hard, and it was daunting, and quite often I would have a feeling in my stomach close to fear or panic when I considered what I'd committed myself to (6 million television viewers in the UK alone was enough to give me stage fright, even if I was going to be running alongside 34,999 other people). Friday nights were a write-off: the bottle of red wine and giant bar of chocolate and late-night film that was my end-of-week celebration did not mix with an early start and double-digit mileage on Saturday mornings. But then I would go out, and start running, and out of nowhere, a motor would splutter to life, or magic would happen.

Sometimes it would be that while I was slogging along painfully I remembered that Grace often felt the same way as she struggled to get to grips with schoolwork, or understand the social cues of her friends, and that she didn't get a day off, or the option to stay at home and eat chocolate on the sofa.

Other times I would reflect on what the money I was raising could do, and feel buoyed by the thought that my efforts would fund help for other worried parents to find advice via the Autism Helpline, or pay for a companion to regularly meet someone who had autism, or give practical support to someone with autism who was looking for work.

Or it might just be that a huge adrenaline rush kicked in. Sometimes I would laugh aloud with joy and sprint and remember that the last antidepressant I took was six months ago.

Those early days of training were excruciating and monotonous and humbling. I often felt overwhelmed as I fought to organise time to do it among work and the children and the daily chores. But it was also the best thing that had ever happened to me. I had a sense of purpose and achievement and a project to be proud of that was mine.

Then somewhere in the weeks around Christmas that changed. I stopped running and I stopped writing about it – by now my blog about life with Grace had attracted a decent number of regular readers. It would be easy to say that it was simply due to the busy time of year, but the break was less to do with the busyness of family activities – the tending to clamouring, hyped-up children that makes the Christmas holiday so particularly unrestful – and more to do with a sudden queasiness that descended whenever I contemplated either activity.

That holiday I couldn't bear to go near the fridge, the source of my discomfort, which hummed carelessly away as though unaware of my torment. It wasn't the groaning shelves of baked meats and ripe cheeses inside that provoked my biliousness, but my training plan, pinned up on the front by an array of colourful magnetic letters. I had abandoned it.

Outside the weather was iron grey and hard cold. The tail end of the month, the last gasp of the year. There was a sense of judgement all around: newspapers, television and online media were full of lists of what had been good and bad in the last twelve months, who and what had succeeded and failed; assessments with the benefit of hindsight confidently outlining past events with a view to foretelling the next. Amid their chatter I judged myself and I found myself wanting. I was a hypocrite and a dissembler. After weeks of extolling the life-changing and life-affirming joys of running with the zeal of the converted I had suddenly stopped running.

And I wasn't quite sure how it had happened.

At first I was under the weather and eased off. Then I was just exhausted, so indulged in a short break. My routine felt overwhelming, so Amelia changed it. Then came a busy period at work for my husband, who notched up so many late nights in his office that it was impossible for me to leave our home full of sleeping children.

Then there was a terrible, terrible treadmill session, when my legs felt like they did not belong to me and would not move to my will, and my throat and chest burned with the effort and still I missed every time target for every mile on my training plan for that day. Soaked in sweat and dismay I thought: this is no longer what's helping me to keep going. It has become another task, another project to juggle along with all the other demands on my time, and another yardstick by which to measure my failings.

We are good at this, we women. In particular, there is a certain kind of mother who does this. When the job is not quite demanding enough, or when circumstances dictate that it must be downgraded, or even halted altogether, when the kids occupy every moment and their accomplishments, needs and desires rotate further up the list of priorities and the food shop and the laundry and the constant tidying and the to-do lists teeter higher and ever higher, the thing that is yours and yours alone – the whatever it is you do to make time for yourself amid the hubbub – becomes the thing that you do to prove to yourself that you still matter. That you've still got it. It becomes the thing that offsets that seam of gnawing constant anxiety, that thread of worry present throughout all the other activities, that voice that says, 'Is this it? Can I do more? Did I fail yet?' Thus the joy and the accomplishment of it turn to ash.

So I stepped off the treadmill. I was not running and all I could think about was running. My not-running guilt was particularly toxic because the running was so interwoven with my maternal responsibilities: the act of putting one foot in front of the other had come to represent progress for Grace too, and when I was not doing it I felt as though the process of supporting her had also ground to a halt. But. When I thought of putting on my running kit, something rebelled and said no, not yet, I'm not ready again yet. On two occasions I managed to get out of the door and jog 6 miles, which felt like utter fakery. According to the schedule on my fridge, I had missed three sessions of hill sprints, three sessions of interval training and nearly three of those stomach-churning long runs – I had not completed 11 miles or 12 miles over the last two Saturdays and was struck with fear to contemplate the 13 miles assigned to the day after tomorrow.

And lo, my body took control of the situation. It succumbed to a thick cold that made my teeth and eye sockets ache, my nose stream constantly, and my legs want no more challenge than that of walking upstairs to bed. Propped against a pile of pillows and huddled under my duvet I shivered, despite the fact that the heating was turned up high enough to make the bedroom radiator groan and clank with effort and beads of condensation trace their way down clouded window panes.

While I hid and waited to get better and to run again, one thing above all else gave me hope. A steady stream of generous donations to my fundraising pot showed me that my family and friends still had faith. Their message that I wouldn't let them down gave me the courage to believe it myself.

Eventually, I felt better and took again to pacing the house worrying about Grace's statement and what the next term held for her. Over the last few days of the holiday the thought of what awaited us both preyed on my mind, making me anxious and irritable. Contemplating the bureaucracy and paperwork that had become our life, and feeling my mental anguish build, the idea of simple physical pain became suddenly appealing again. And I knew I had to prepare myself to endure.

So I went running. Up a very steep hill. In the wind and rain and isolation of a dark grey morning under lowering skies. I was staying at my parents' house just outside Sheffield, on the edges of the Peak District, and I selected the worst part of an occasional circuit I ran whenever I was there: a winding climb that had defeated me on many occasions in the past.

Twenty times I ran up that hill. To begin with I ran fast, full of tension and anger. Then I ran more steadily, grimly repetitive. Then I began to weave and stagger a little bit, and shout aloud my frustration. A few sheep looked up. The wind continued to blow hard against me. Several petrified trees dotted along the brow of the ascent struck attitudes of cowed wintry defeat. I huffed and puffed downhill between each attempt, counting in my head the remaining efforts as I reached the bottom, braced and once again flung myself back up the way I'd come. By the end I was almost hysterical, giggling inside my laced-tight hood at the sight I must have presented and listening to the rasp of my sleeves against my sides as I tried to power myself along using my arms as pistons.

After forty-five minutes I had achieved my goal and taken the first steps towards being mentally and physically stronger for the challenges that awaited me when term started again on Monday morning, when I would take Grace back to school. I had also remembered that this road was a long one and that there would always be new hills in front of me. The trick was to use them to make me stronger. And not to think about them too much. Sometimes you just have to keep putting one foot in front of the other, I told myself.

Over the next few weeks I threw myself into training with renewed vigour. I didn't give myself time to think about what I was doing or to feel anxious or grumpy about it. I just did it, going up a gear from easy 6-mile runs to more difficult 10-mile runs and then starting to steadily, grimly add on a mile every week to that during my long run, in the hope that the rest of the week's training was building my muscles and my stamina. Sometimes it was fine. Sometimes it was difficult. And sometimes it was simply awful. I just had to keep going and to use the bad times to make me stronger. I rose at 6 a.m. to fit sessions in before work and I ran at 9 p.m. to fit them in afterwards. I snuck off when Betty went for her afternoon nap at weekends and my husband supervised the older ones on Saturday mornings so I could do my long, looping runs around north London. I discovered new parks and cycle routes and ramblers' trails. My trainers were clagged with mud. The washing machine turned constantly with my sweaty clothes.

One morning I woke up feeling something wasn't right. I wiggled my toes experimentally and cudgelled my brain into thought. Around me the dim shapes of bedroom furniture came into focus as the light outside the windows diluted darkness into grey grain.

It was Saturday. A 14-mile run beckoned. I swallowed hard, and discovered what else had been troubling me: a seam of pain down the back of my throat and between my ears, that tell-tale sign spelling the start of another cold. I sat up and felt my chest tighten, my head thump uncomfortably.

There was no question of not running. This was the start of the next leg up; the move into real marathon running, the advance from the known of 13 miles into the unknown of 14 and the first proper test of my endurance for several months.

I pulled on my clothes and ate breakfast with my ears ringing, the porridge sticking in curdled lumps to my tender stomach lining.

From the moment I set foot outside I knew it was going to be all, all wrong.

I set off along the road on which I live, avoiding the wobbly paving slabs without conscious thought now, then turned right past the bus stop, down the hill under the railway bridge and then up and up and over the crest, a two-minute climb that usually defrosted my joints and set my blood singing. This time it was as though I had swallowed a press of angry wasps that teemed and chafed in my chest, buzzing in my throat with every huff. Arriving at the top of the hill in agony, I paced on for a couple of moments with no heed to my surroundings as my thoughts fought each other. The urge to give up was immense. The fear of the psychological impact this could have on me was equally huge. I had never given up on a run before. I had never stopped running during a run before: just to slow to a walk would be admitting defeat and creating a dangerous template for the following attempt and the one after that and the one after that and so on . . .

So I continued. I had planned an 8-mile route with a 3-mile loop at each end, drawn in my head like a weightlifter's bar and discs. The weight of it was crushing.

I had gone 2 miles and was round the path into the woods when a small white terrier dashed out of a thicket 50 yards ahead and made for me. I slowed my already treacly pace and feinted left to dodge the dog. It bobbed briefly the wrong way then bounced back, barking shrilly, and came straight for me, leaping up on to my thighs and aiming a nip at my face. I reeled back, stumbled, then tried to run faster, only to entice it further. The dog chased me for the next ten or twenty paces while I, like a drunk, aimed ineffective blows and curses at it. Its owner stood watching, carefully blank-faced, a way off. I gritted my teeth, put my head down and produced a spurt of speed that was enough to break the game and leave the mutt behind. Turning to check it had given up, I ran backwards briefly, aiming a last volley of abuse at the owner, then headed into the next stretch of path.

I had run 3 miles and my legs felt like water. I was dressed for the cold and soaked in sweat: over the next 3 miles I removed my hat, then my gloves and my coat, which I tied around my waist. I must have looked like a stumbling mad woman, scarlet and wild-eyed among sedate Saturday joggers and couples out for an amble in the unseasonal sunshine. The pain in my chest was like a saw.

At 7 miles I emerged from a park and began the slow climb up the next hill, a very public torture along a path at the side of a busy road. My arrival at this section coincided with the return of the ten o'clock riding lesson to the stables on the other side of the road and I found myself at the end of a line of horses and riders, a swaying single-file column stretching for ten or twelve steeds which proceeded with regal slowness in front of me. I did not have the strength or space to speed up and overtake them in the narrow gap between path and traffic, so for five minutes I staggered behind, skipping steaming piles of horse shit and acknowledging toots from drivers like the clown at the end of a carnival parade.

Finally they were gone, I was at the top of the hill and a mile of downhill rural joy via scenic fields awaited. I had reached the 8-mile point, the magic gateway at which I usually get my second wind and enjoy several miles of easy loose-limbed running. This time nothing happened. I crawled on.

I spent the following 4 miles drifting in and out of consciousness and marvelling through the pain at my marvellous legs and their marvellous ability to somehow keep going, albeit at a granny-stagger. At one point I was tempted to take a photograph of my feet in their filthy, mud-caked trainers. Such dear, comfortable trainers. I was like a student taking hallucinogens for the first time and goggling at the sudden quotidian wonders that revealed themselves.

At 12 miles it started to rain.

At 13.3 miles a hiccup of self-pity escaped me and I cried, briefly.

I flailed through the next point-seven miles with my wrist in front of my face, willing the blinking digital numbers on my watch to reach their final sum more quickly.

And then it was done. My legs were in agony, my chest was on fire, my scalp and hair were sodden. With shaking hands I turned the key in my front door, staggered into the kitchen and started to cry. It was over, but I knew I had to do it again and again, whether or not it got easier, which at that point seemed entirely impossible.

Gracie, my darling, I thought: I have often wondered what your days are like and how you summon such reserves of courage and grit to keep going when everything seems difficult and the barriers constant, one after another. This, I felt, had been a closer glimpse. I stood, still braced against the table where we ate our family meals, and wondered again at my daughter, flooded with love and admiration for her.

Not long afterwards Grace's trials showed me again how far I still was from sharing her pain.

The new term had been relatively quiet so far, although Grace had often had trouble sleeping for worry about what might happen next. She had returned from a holiday with her father taller, happy in herself and relaxed. After spending Christmas with me she went to Ireland, kicking up her heels and over the traces; all routine gone in exchange for a round of cheers and songs and jokes and music and up all hours and smoky rooms and go on just another one and well now, Gracie, I'd say you've grown, from endless rounds of relatives. She was returned to me paler and shattered, wearily elegant: wearing dark circles under her eyes and purple varnish on her fingernails.

She'd had three weeks of presents, parties and time away from school. This sense of unreality was hard for her to shake off – not least because an element of it was always present for her, even on her most grounded and formulaic school-and-home-for-tea days. My first mention of piano practice was met with a shriek – head tilted back, eyes screwed shut – and a 'NO!' and fists hammering on the chair. Later on a request that homework be finished was more calmly received, but still the eyes rolled and nostrils flared; there was a pretty stamp of her foot. I breathed in and out and said calm things inside my head. It's a careful, slow process, this reeling her in and tethering her back down at the end of the holidays, and I sympathised with her reluctance.

One night, not long before school started, I decided to have an early night with her and, going upstairs, encountered her in the bathroom, pacing and talking to herself. I sent her to bed. A little while later I looked into her bedroom. Then I climbed the ladder up to her bed, where she lay stiffly, faking sleep beneath her eye mask. I could see only her nose and the tense set of her mouth.

'Come on,' I said gently. 'It's time to get ready to go back to it now.'

She winced as if I had struck her.

'But, Mummy,' she said, 'I don't want to go back. I don't want to go back to school and all the arguments and getting people annoyed.'

'You don't have to go back to that,' I said. 'They're getting better at understanding you and I'm going to make sure that they keep getting better.'

'But –' she bit her lip. 'What about X?' She named her latest persecutor.

'Don't worry about X,' I said. 'The teachers know she's playing up and they're watching her. Now, we're going to have a lovely weekend. We'll have lots of cuddles and kisses and rest and relaxing. We'll have good food and good sleep – and if you sleep you'll be much better at keeping your temper and being patient and able to concentrate.'

Grace exhaled a long breath, slowly.

'OK. But will you sing me a song, Mummy? Please?'

So I sang her a song, the same song that I have shushed her

to sleep with for years. I leaned over and put one arm around her and cradled her, while I murmured the words of the lullaby across her skin: along her forehead and into her hairline; into the pale gleam of her ear, down along her petal-smooth cheek to her jawline and along to her soft mouth, which I kissed as I sang: 'Go to sleep, my baby, Close your pretty eyes, Angels are above you, Peeping at you, darling, from the skies.' I stroked her hair and traced the length of her nose. 'Great big moon is shining, Stars begin to peep, Time for little Gracie to go to sleep, Time for Gracie to go to sleep.'

Her mouth curved in a faint smile. Her body had relaxed.

'Goodnight, Grace,' I said.

'Goodnight, Mummy,' she answered. 'I love you.'

The next evening, at around the same time, I checked on Grace. She was still awake and asked me if I would sing to her again. She shuffled over to the edge of her bed so that I could put my arms around her again. Before I started to sing, she angled her head up, estimating the position of my face – she was again wearing her eye mask and the blindness of her action rendered her entirely fragile and vulnerable – seeking to tell me something.

She said: 'I've decided I'm really looking forward to the start of school, Mummy. There will be loads of interesting things to do before we get stuck into the boring old schoolwork and I'm thinking, hey, it will be good!'

The forced enthusiasm and bravery in her voice skewered me. I sang to her and I was glad that she couldn't see my face. I sang to her with my voice cracking and my eyes filling up with tears. I thought how courageous she was and how endlessly optimistic. I thought of the baby she was when I whispered her to sleep with this song. I thought of the toddler and the little, little girl she was. I thought of Betty in her room across the landing, pink and flushed, cocooned in sleep and smelling of bubble bath, who also now asked me to sing her the same song. I thought of the gulf between my two girls and feared for the differences in the lives they would lead and I tilted my head back as I sang so that the tears did not spill.

When I was finished Grace murmured sleepily: 'Just one more time please, Mummy.'

I swallowed hard and started singing again.

A couple of weeks later I got a phone call from the school to tell me my daughter had been involved in a fight. Tagged 'it' in a game she neither understood nor wanted to play – the kids all covered in charcoal after art class – she recoiled at an unexpected, smudgy touch, and pushed the other child away, hard. He pushed her harder, so she hit him. So he punched her, hard. So she kicked him, equally hard. Then they flew at each other's faces. By the time the teacher intervened they were on the floor surrounded by classmates chanting 'fight, fight, fight'.

Whenever I talked about the bullying of Grace with other parents of autistic children their advice was: call in the police, get a lawyer, home-school her if possible. Just get her out.

But it wasn't that simple. I couldn't home-school Grace because I couldn't afford not to work. I couldn't take her out of the education system because we were in the middle of applying for a statement of educational needs and we had to have it by the time we completed our secondary schools applications the following October. Otherwise she would have to go to the local comprehensive and get eaten alive. I couldn't afford a tutor for her if she was not in school. By now I had written formally and informally and met in person Grace's headteacher on many occasions. There was an understanding on both sides that the bullying was unacceptable and must stop. Nearly all the parents of all the children in Grace's class had been called in to the school at some point or other, or so it seemed to me. But the teachers could not supervise every child at every minute. And so still the bullying continued.

I didn't know what to do. On Wednesday I collected my daughter, listened to her and held her. I went to bed feeling an utter failure.

On Thursday I went to work. Because of course I still had to do my other job. My employers at this point had agreed that I could work from home two days a week in order to be able to attend the various Grace-related meetings. On the days I went to the office I travelled by Tube to the heart of London's financial district. On those days my hair was clean and my face made-up. On the surface I was a professional, if you overlooked the bags under my eyes and the inky 'to-do' lists scribbled on the backs of my hands where I couldn't forget or lose them. Once, I adored my job: it took me around the world, introduced me to leaders of government and people who shaped lives. I held the privilege of news no one yet knew scattered like diamond dust through my notebooks, and delighted in writing the first stories to share it, watching my headlines unfurl across the bottom of television and computer screens. These days, I sat at a desk and checked other people's copy and waited for the next reorganisation to move me down to the next rung. On Thursday I learned details of the next reorganisation, in which I was to be moved down to the next rung.

On Friday morning, wretched and full of bile, I provoked a humdinger of a row with my husband, lifting the lid on weeks of patient endurance on his part and airing noxious, festering tensions. There was screaming and slammed doors and Betty, sobbing and scared, looking from one of us to the other in big-eyed bewildered fright.

I spent the day with the beat of one question in my head. That evening I got home again, ran a bath, got in and wondered again how to do away with myself.

That day – the culmination of weeks of frenzied worry and pain – it felt as though a sudden stillness had finally descended and an answer had presented itself, beautiful in its simplicity.

So that evening I thought: I'll just take myself away. I can't do anything. In all areas of my life I have failed. With the demented clarity that comes with that final decision I told myself: they'll all be better off without me. I sat for a very long time wondering how best to go about it. Several times the water cooled and I refilled the bath until the temperature nearly made me faint. Scalded pink, cleansed, refreshed, I thought: pills would be best. I could just lie down and sleep it all away.

Then I thought – wait. I can't. I've got to run 15 miles tomorrow.

Such was the mad logic of the discourse going around my head that it was not my darling children – my Grace, who needed so much, and Betty, so little and lovely and freshly pressed – nor my husband or family (my sister, expecting me at her birthday party the next evening) who claimed my senses and clawed me back to the business of living.

No, it was that I had to run. Or else I would have failed that too. Running was as yet the only thing that I could still do successfully and I had to cling to it.

On realising that I had to keep going, I started to cry again. But I got out of the bath and dried myself and put on my pyjamas and went to bed with only my dinner in my stomach in order to wake up again the next day.

The next morning, I ran 15 miles. I left my headphones and my music at home. For nearly three hours I listened to the sound of my breathing going in and out and the splash of my feet in mud and the cawing of rooks in the trees over my head. I came to no astonishing conclusions, nor did my meditation show me the light and the way. I don't know whether it restored my sanity completely. But it did remind me that there was something I could still do and that perhaps I was stronger than I thought.

That weekend, running saved my life.

13

Back to school

We went to look at secondary schools for Grace.

To be specific, we went to look at the schools we thought would be the best places for Grace, while we prayed that the statement would be approved.

We did not visit our nearest institution, a recently built academy with a reputation for strict discipline, emphasis on good grades and, according to playground parental gossip, a steady stream of weeping, pressured teachers in the head-teacher's office. Nor did we visit the prestigious girls' school cited by so many parents as their reason for moving to our part of north London: the demands of its entrance exam effectively excluded Grace regardless of her other abilities.

Here yet again I found my life diverging from the one I had imagined after kids. Raised in a family of teachers and academics where the emphasis had always been on achievement and superior intellect, I had always planned for my children to be part of an academic elite. Top school, top grades, strict rules and Oxford or Cambridge. Instead now the thought of sending my daughter to one of these disciplinarian blue-stocking establishments made my blood run cold. She would be terrified and frozen in the face of rigid demands relating to behaviour and schoolwork.

But she was so bright, my girl. Her fizzing, clever brain held all sorts of secrets that we had not yet unlocked and I could not bear to think of her academic possibilities being shut down because one school had failed to find a way to teach her.

I wondered where to find a broader, looser environment with scope for Grace to relax and explore her creative talents while hopefully also discovering others that I suspected she had locked away because of a wrongful belief that she was stupid. I couldn't figure out, however, how a school might marry this provision and also provide the steady daily guidance she still needed. And I worried that anywhere young children felt free to express themselves might mean them freely expressing their opinions of Grace in a way that could hurt her again.

I asked lots of parents and educational advisers and the name of one school in particular kept coming up. I made an appointment and went along with Grace's dad to look at it. I had not heard of this school, particularly. It was not one of the ones that parents discussed in hushed, semi-excited tones. I tried to clear my mind of prejudice and open my eyes.

The building was dazzling in its whiteness and made me squint. Rising ahead long and square, framed by brand-new dark-tarred playgrounds and mint-green grass and dotted sculptures it looked more like a German museum of architecture than a secondary school. We walked up to it along a broad, flat passageway, blinking.

Inside, we were greeted by the head of the Additional Educational Needs department, a woman with an intense regard under bushy eyebrows and a sudden, charming smile. She asked us a bit about Grace, nodded briefly as we told her, then explained precisely what Grace needed and how the school would provide it in terms of teaching support, playground assistance, mentoring and counselling. She talked about the school's team of autism experts and learning-support assistants, buddy schemes and homework and lunch clubs. As she spoke, I could feel tears of gratitude and relief rising and had to will them away, making fists of my hands in my pockets in order to maintain my composure.

We walked around the school and saw its drama and art studios, the music rooms and the theatre and the library. Grace's dad and I, no longer adversaries, kept trying not to look at each other and smile. It was like touring your dream home and having to suppress the urge to ask then and there for the keys.

As we left, our guide shook our hands and wished us luck with the local authority and told us to keep in touch. As we were not in the catchment area for the school Grace could only be considered for a place if she was awarded a statement.

Her father and I sat in his car outside the school gates and gazed through the windscreen unseeing for some time afterwards. There was everything and nothing to say. The statement was everything, or else there was nothing.

Later I shared my frustrations with Ethan's father Chris, who agreed:

'It is a ridiculously rigid system,' he said. 'Get one and you're sorted: pick your favourite school. Don't get one, and you've got no rights at all, even if you have a child with proven special needs, even if you're only yards outside the catchment area for the school you want.'

Refused a statement and turned down on the grounds of strict catchment rules by the local school they thought best for their four-year-old son, Chris and his wife took the decision to send him to a private primary school where he is supported by a one-to-one teaching assistant four mornings a week, as well as a speech therapist and an occupational therapy session once a week.

'It costs us £12,000 a year for the school and £7,000 for the extras. We are as poor as we were twenty years ago and we are agonising about what to do next,' Chris said. 'The school is already saying that if he doesn't get a statement by Year 3, the current situation won't work for them. They're a business with the aim of getting their kids into the very best secondary schools and they're brutal with any kid who doesn't cut it academically.

'We'll probably move house into the catchment area of the good primary school that we couldn't get into. It will be cripplingly expensive in housing costs, but less expensive than the school fees. It's a huge job to work it all out.'

Mindful of the alternative if we cannot win a place for our daughter at the school we have just visited, her father and I go to see a private school with a reputation for encouraging free thinkers in a relaxed teaching environment. There is no uniform here and pupils call teachers by their first names. Set up on the edge of Hampstead Heath by radical Victorians as a 'rational' school where children could learn to be independent learners, it also has a large, airy art studio, one of the oldest school photography departments in the country and an excellent drama department and theatre. We tour the clutch of buildings with the registrar, observing the small class sizes, the intimate clusters of comfortable-looking armchairs set up for English tutorials and short lines of stools in the science labs. The neat group of children in the geography class look both alert and relaxed. We pass a band practising in one of the music rooms and peer into a window later on to see the sixth-form common room where young men shoot pool and swap jokes. Last year the school pupils together built a boat, which is in dry dock for the winter, the registrar tells us proudly.

This time Grace's dad and I cannot look at each other for fear. It would cost us £15,000 a year to send Grace to this haven. If she does not get a statement, we would have to pay extra again for her to have the support she needs as the school explains that it does not have the resources to fit additional educational help around more than one subject per child. We are cautioned that the emphasis on independent research and learning may not suit a child who can fixate on some subjects and reject others entirely.

As we walk out we have an edgy conversation about where we would find the money and whether in fact this place would look after Grace.

I go to work and sit watching my talented colleagues, reflecting on the combined brain power there is in this one office, and I wonder what will become of my darling, brilliant daughter. The struggle to find the right school for her has become a battle for her future. It's a battle other mums in my situation know well, and we exchange frustrated tweets and emails across the online forums in which such friendships are forged.

'There was little choice. There is inadequate provision in our locality for those who tend towards the higher functioning side of autism and Aspergers,' said Sarah, aged forty-three and mother to Adrian who is thirteen. 'There is a moderate-learning-difficulties school and schools for those with severe disabilities, but otherwise those with high-functioning autism or Aspergers tend to have to manage in mainstream with support, or not.'

In Adrian's case the 'or not' applied. Overwhelmed by the experience of being in a mainstream school and without the statement that could provide the resources to support him, he developed mental-health problems and stopped going to school. For two years Sarah battled to persuade her local education authority to reassess the child they had once rejected. Eventually, two years after Adrian was diagnosed, a statement of special educational needs was awarded and the family secured a place for him at a specialist school.

Listening to this story I remember the fear of going to secondary school. I remember being twelve, rattling around a poorly modernised red-brick Victorian cathedral and being constantly terrified of being pushed down the stairs or spat upon or grabbed in the toilets. I remember being too tall to be inconspicuous and too geeky to come up with funny replies for my tormentors. I remember thinking: I have to just wait this out until the next lot of new kids arrives next year.

I cannot imagine how I would have felt if someone had told me that the social misery of break time would endure for my entire school life and that classes, books and languages and learning, rather than providing respite, would be a further source of stress and confusion.

Around this time, an article in my National Autistic Society magazine caught my eye. It was a review of a book called *Raising Martians: From Crash-Landing to Leaving Home*, written by a young man with Asperger's Syndrome and designed to guide parents through primary and secondary school from the perspective and needs of their AS children.

I ordered the book, and I emailed its author, asking if he would talk to me personally about his experiences so that I could prepare the way for Grace. What he told me made me even more determined that she should not suffer the same.

When Joshua Muggleton started secondary school aged eleven, he observed a classmate receive a punishment of detention in the first week for forgetting to bring a textbook. Horrified by the prospect of potentially breaking a rule in this way, he resolved to pack every textbook, every workbook, every piece of paper and take everything to school with him every day. Using his locker was not an option because it was situated on the main corridor along which 2000 students bumped and shouted every day – an even more terrifying experience for a child with Asperger's Syndrome. He was instantly a target.

To this day Joshua, now twenty-two, wears the imprint of that school trauma in his bearing, slouched forward because of the weight he continually carried.

'After six weeks at secondary school I became depressed and by Christmas was making active attempts to take my own life because the bullying was so bad and the teachers didn't know why I was having such severe problems,' he told me. 'Eventually, around Year 10, I started to have meltdowns. I'd wake up on a school day and I'd start having panic attacks. I'd have to psych myself up for fifteen minutes to get out of the car and get into school. So I stopped going to school.'

Joshua is now studying for a degree in clinical psychology at St Andrews University. He gives talks about having Asperger's Syndrome as well as having written *Raising Martians*. He chats easily, and is polite and funny and self-deprecating. That he was once a child traumatised by the education system is remarkable. The explanation he gives for his experiences is depressingly familiar even ten years later: a late diagnosis combined with a school that was uninterested in understanding what Josh's labels meant.

After several attempts to get him back into school (allowing him to drop some subjects and leave earlier in the afternoons than his classmates) failed owing to the constant bullying and lack of understanding, Joshua was signed off school on medical grounds. He then spent several vital learning years at home, scared to leave the house in case he saw someone from school, and struggling to keep up with his academic learning by way of internet tutorials. Going back to school to take his exams provoked another nervous breakdown.

Eventually, he secured a place at a specialist further education college at which he had been engaged to give one of his talks. With the right help and understanding Joshua studied maths, business studies and psychology – which he found 'easy'. The discovery that he could go to university came as a jolt.

'I realised in my second year of A-level study that I was going to get enough points to go to university. It shocked me. I hadn't registered what that meant. My grades at school had always been so poor that I didn't think I'd be able to get A levels. When I saw my results I felt numb.'

Listening to Josh I am relieved to hear his happy ending, and also terrified all over again by the tightrope Grace and I must walk. One slip, one wobble, one unlucky step and that day of achievement – those hugs and smiles and whoops and celebrations in front of the school noticeboard that have become a staple of news broadcast footage every year on publication of exam results – falls away from us.

Josh's final words of advice to me ring in my ears: 'Pick the school carefully. Try to make sure it's the right size and the right ethos. Get a support plan in place before your child starts so that you have the benefit of a smooth transition. It's important to get it right in the first few weeks rather than letting it go wrong and solving it.'

Talk of this 'transition' period pops up regularly now. Grace's support workers – the army of people who now like me are waiting, fingers crossed, to see if our paperwork mountain has sufficiently impressed the local authority – also tell me how important it will be to introduce Grace to her new school over time so that she can grow accustomed to the unfamiliar demands on her. While I wait to know whether I can send my daughter to the school we so very much want, I ask other parents how they prepared their children during this time.

'My advice would be to find out as much as you can about the school and what to expect. We spent a lot of the summer holidays talking to John about some of the changes he should expect at secondary school,' said Lynne, who is forty-eight and stepmum to John, now aged fourteen. 'We tried to develop his problem-solving skills and gave him a number of scenarios to work through, like, "What would you do if you were lost? What would you do if you didn't understand the homework you were set?"'

The transfer from primary to secondary school was still difficult, Lynne told me, as John got to grips with a big, new building, crowded corridors and lots of different teachers: 'There were occasions when he refused to leave the house or get out of the car on a school morning.'

However, I took heart again from another positive ending. 'We feel that John has been given similar support and chances as other pupils at the school. In most subjects he is now working at an expected level for his age, and in some cases is exceeding expectations. So I would say that he is being given the opportunity to achieve his potential,' Lynne concluded.

*

At this point I decided I must prepare for success instead of anticipating failure. My next running challenge was near and while I waited – and waited and waited – to hear from the education experts what they had decided for Grace, the running seemed like a good place to try out my new approach.

I had entered the Brighton half-marathon with the aim of beating my Royal Parks time and increasing both my pace and my confidence ahead of London.

But once the race started I found it was not that straight-forward.

It's a Sunday morning, blue and beautiful and absolutely bloody freezing.

It is the kind of morning when, if you are not a runner, you might pull on boots and a hat and walk the dog while exclaiming at the freshly washed skies and the crispness beneath your feet, before letting yourself gratefully back into a warm house with a tingling numbness in your lips and nose.

It is the kind of morning when, if you are not a runner, you might meet a friend for a bracing stomp up a hill in the coun-tryside, cut short with exclamations that it's actually really very cold, and followed by a gravy-splashed pub lunch and a snooze in front of the fire.

If you are not a runner, you will sample this bright, icy day with pleasure made all the more intense for knowing that you need not be out in it long.

I am a runner, so I am still out in this day. I am bowed into it like a penitent waiting to be told of absolution, bearing the lash of a bitter wind as I move my lips in silent prayer to make it stop soon.

At least I am not alone. Alongside and in front and behind me a mass of people also bob and groan – 9999 other people participating in this half-marathon along the ruthlessly exposed seafront.

It is becoming apparent that I have got this all wrong. I am not enjoying myself. I have completed around a third of my usual weekend run and yet I feel off kilter, off the pace, stiff and creaky. There is a recurring, uncomfortable twang at the top of my left leg.

I know the reason I have screwed this up: I am running too slowly for fear of running too fast. The last time I ran a half-marathon I got terribly excited halfway through and then almost collapsed before the finish, spent from a 4-mile sprint in the middle of the race when the atmosphere and the crowds and the sense of imminent achievement soused me like cheap wine and left me staggering and gurning at the end of the party.

So this time I started at the back. Way, way at the back. Partly, I think, because I was also overawed by the companion with whom I walked to the start line: the husband of a friend who runs this race regularly; a mass of muscle and sinew who is used to knocking off one of these events in around an hour and twenty minutes and is so tough he's wearing a singlet and shorts today.

Meanwhile, I am wedged behind two women who have chatted non-stop since the start (the fact that I am not out of breath either is not really a comfort at this point) and a

man who is dressed as a tap. We pass only occasional supporters – we are way out past the marina now and the crowds
are thin here. We all trot past a tall woman standing on the
verge who is wearing a hat like a chimney stove and waving
a giant Union Jack and occasionally honking an ancient
brass horn to encourage us onwards. Poop, poop! she honks
at us beaming, then spots the man at my side. 'Come on!'
she shouts in plummy tones. 'Come on, Mister – what are
you? A pipe? Come on, Mister Pipe!' Poop, poop! Beside
me I can see the man's face tighten with irritation.

At this point I check myself and look at my watch. I am
running alongside a man in a tap outfit and it has taken me
approximately ten minutes longer than it should have to
complete 6 miles. I am going to have to get a move on at this
rate if I am to come anywhere near the time I completed in
my last race.

I lengthen my stride. I have trained for this. I am supposed
to be taking this race on, not letting it frighten me into
submission.

As soon as I start running properly my body starts to relax
and my mind tightens up: I switch on my iPod to drown out
the little anxious hand-wringer inside my head who is saying,
you shouldn't be doing this, you might not make it, what if
you run out of steam like last time?

Tra la la, I tell it, and turn the music up a bit louder.

Then I spot a woman in front of me who is wearing a
co-ordinated pink tracksuit and giant headphones. She
has a massive rope of hair down her back and is accompanied by one man who has 'COACH' emblazoned across

his back, and another who keeps sprinting ahead to film her with his phone. I draw alongside and see a face with thick, dark Disneyesque lashes and a hue of orange never found in nature.

I think: I can run this race faster than Katie Price, and I speed up and pass her, leaving both her and the grimacing maiden aunt in my head, flapping her hands in agitation, far behind.

By now I'm running past beach huts in primary colours and smiling families waving and cheering – and look! There's mine, briefly, looking cold and as though they'd like that gravy-splashed lunch some time soon – and I've got 3 miles to go and I'm passing people left and right and it doesn't hurt. I can feel the muscles in my legs and the strength in my arms as I push on and this is new, this is not what it felt like before – this is a stronger, fitter me.

Two miles on and my legs feel tighter and I am becoming more conscious of the deep gulps of air I am taking. I need to adjust my stride. I hesitate for a moment then test out a faster pace: it works.

As I run the last 800 yards and bound over the finish line I feel like yelling with joy and frustration. I complete the race in exactly the same time as my first half-marathon but the two experiences could not be more different. This has been a lesson in learning to trust my ability: the training is working. I decide to sign up for a 20-mile race in four weeks' time. I need to try again to get the pacing right. London is in eight weeks.

Later, when I am showered and dressed, I present Grace

with my medal: a chunky pewter square strung on a red ribbon which reads: 'FINISHER'.

She looks at it in dismay then looks up at me and asks: 'Mummy, did you come last?'

'No,' I tell her. 'No chance.'

Full of fresh excitement about my abilities I bounded into the next phase of my training with new resolve. I was no longer going to play it safe. I was not going to plod along at the back of the crowd. I was going to really run, damn it.

The next long training run was an epiphany. Rather than hiding my James Bond GPS watch under my sleeve to ignore it and try to forget the distance I had to run – I would cautiously peer at it after sixteen songs, or the third hill, and hope to be pleasantly surprised by how little I had left to do – I used it to monitor and improve my performance. (Cue chorus from the run-o-sphere: well, DUH!) Holding myself to a strict time target for each mile: checking my watch and not allowing myself a gentle jogging breather at the top of inclines or a more stately pace across uneven fields, I sliced almost four minutes from my half-marathon time and continued to keep pace for a further 2 miles.

I felt jubilation at hitting 15 miles in two and a half hours, swiftly followed by extreme pain. It wasn't agony, not quite. The top of my left leg – that peculiar little twang from the week before – had developed into something so sore that I couldn't walk or stretch without grimacing. So I walked, stretched, took a long bath and decided to ignore it.

The next day I went to the gym and did lots of lunges and

squats. The day after that I ran 7 miles in a whisker over an hour. The evening after that the pain in my leg was so bad that I asked my trainer for advice, batting away flutters of panic as I did so. She asked me lots of precise questions. Then she said she thought I had tendonitis. The cure: stop all running, entirely, immediately, for six to eight weeks. Unless you're in the last seven weeks of training for a marathon.

I took two days of rest, iced my leg, stretched it, submitted to an embarrassing (if rather lovely) sports massage. I bought anti-inflammatory drugs, pain-relief rub, magnesium muscle spray, 'mobility' bath salts and a waist-high stack of power bars to give me extra strength. I tried not to think about it too much. I thought about it all the time.

The evening before my next long run – the 17 miles circled on my training programme – I ate chicken, brown rice and a mixture of peas, leeks, broad beans and spinach. That night, I counted every grain and pulse back out again, bent groaning in the bathroom through the wee small hours as a virus struck. My husband, similarly afflicted, and I shuffled in and out of that room for the next twenty-four hours like the figures on a Swiss clock (BARF! It's three o' clock!), then spent the following twenty-four hours immobile and moaning.

It took me another week before I could look at food without blanching, or contemplate any exercise. Throughout that time my leg throbbed steadily. Eventually, I looked again at my training plan and saw that the next day I had to go and do sprints for an hour or so. I should have been in the hardest and most intense period of my marathon training. Instead I felt like my fourteen-year-old self when school sports day came round with its weary inevitability: how am I going to get through this without revealing the depths of my uselessness?

But then an envelope arrived. I opened it and read the letter within, and put it on my desk, propped against the bulging file of documents about my daughter. The letter was from the council and advised me that they would meet to consider my daughter's case in four weeks' time. They named the date on which a group of strangers would take five minutes to consider our request for help. It was all the reminder that I needed of why I was in training. I packed my bag and went to the gym.

I got through the next few training sessions somehow. I still felt light-headed and nauseous and not at my best. But I pushed the worry away and kept going. Training helped me to deal with the waiting. By now it was just under five weeks until the London Marathon – peak training time – and my fundraising pot for the National Autistic Society brimmed with generous donations. I was very conscious, however, that the combination of illness and injury had set me back a vital week or so. The 20-mile race I'd entered was also coming up fast. I had to hit 18 miles on my next long run in order to stay on track.

I've described some rough sessions in the course of this journey. None of them come anywhere near the horror show of that 18-mile run. By mile six I felt so ill that for the first time I seriously considered stopping and going home. The twang of tendonitis was slight, and bearable. But I was oppressed by a persistent queasiness that made it an effort to remain upright. Twice I was overtaken by an old man in long white socks and lean brown legs, clearly an old habitué of the rural route I had mapped out thinking I could suffer in private. I forced an energy bar down me, gagging and spluttering. I abandoned my headphones: music wasn't distracting me. It felt like trying to listen to the radio over the sound of drilling. Just before mile fifteen what had been a hint of lower back pain – a niggle, a thought that I'd need a good stretch there once I got home – suddenly roared into life. I ran the next 2 miles bent and crablike, tears of frustration and fright on my face as every step with my right leg sent knives of agony through my spine. Every ounce of willpower I had took me only as far as 17.1 miles at which point I stopped, racked by sobs that continued long after the physical pain had abated. For the first time ever I had failed to finish.

My trainer banned me from all further exercise until I had a formal diagnosis.

So then I went to see an osteopath. I had not slept for almost a week by that point, kept awake by the knives and the fear of finding out that I could no longer run. (There was one thing worse than running the London Marathon, I discovered, and it was the prospect of not running the London Marathon.) Weary and apprehensive, I went to see Gavin Burt, an erect, compact man with a firm handshake. He greeted me, assessed me, then lay me down and mapped me with his practitioner's fingers. He diagnosed sacroiliac joint dysfunction – the bit of my tail bone that connected to my pelvis was askew and jammed tight on the right-hand side.

The good news: he could fix it, in around four weeks. The bad news: I must not run until he had fixed it. I lay on the treatment table leaking more tears into my hair as I looked at the ceiling and took in the weight of his diagnosis. The next time I would be able to attempt double-digit mileage would be on 22 April.

To take my mind off that wait, I returned to the other one. The day before Grace's case was to be heard I telephoned her case officer to ask how soon the next day we would have a decision and how soon I could contact him to find it out. Another member of the team picked up and told me that the man I sought was on holiday, and not back until next week. She told me I could look for him again then. I began to see this man, another key player in this farce who again I had never met, as the Scarlet Pimpernel – at each call or visit from me flinging himself out of a window or shimmying down a tree, to escape in a coach and four.

I knew Grace's future was in the balance. For her, the outcome would mean the difference between two lives. A yes – and agreement to conduct a statutory assessment of her situation – would be vital progress towards a formal agreement to provide extra learning resources, her own learning assistant and a place at that school, the one her dad and I had visited, and loved. Her world would open up again, her fear of new subjects and social situations diminish. It put me in mind of the film *Sliding Doors*. In one scenario, the train doors would open and Grace would be allowed to walk out into a happy ending. In the other, she would be confined to an endless, dreary round of stops and starts and airless confinement, boiling with frustration and sadness at the limitations of her surroundings.

I couldn't bear to think about what we'd do if they said no, there's no case here.

I wanted to fret and fidget and panic. I wanted to talk, endlessly, about how frightened I was and what would we do if they wouldn't assess Grace and how would I look after her and how could I find a good school for her and how would I do the marathon and what if I had to walk it and what if I had to crawl?

Instead I breathed steadily. In through the nose, out through the mouth. Running had taught me this. If you panic on tough terrain you are done for. Instead I put my shoulders back and I tensed down to the core of me, feeling the strength I had built up, and I kept waiting, gradually, minute by minute, until, again, I found I could endure.

14

Grace grows up

There is cherry blossom on the trees in the park and the ducks have emerged from their nests among the reeds by the pond, quacking loudly to demand bread from passers-by. They pick their way along the bank with an odd high-stepping consideration for the purple buds of crocuses beneath their orange toes.

Two weeks have passed. From my seat outside the café I watch Grace run among her friends. In the last few months she has shot up again, and the hem of her school tunic skims above her knees exposing long, long legs. She is laughing as she runs, hair flying, eyes bright. The weather is warm and she has cast off her coat. It lies on the seat beside me, along-side that of Betty, who sits at my other side eating an ice-cream the size of her head and giving me a running commentary on the process.

'I've got a strawberry one,' says Betty, affectionately patting the top of her Cornetto and then licking the tips of her fingers. 'Look, Mummy. It's a strawberry one. It's very sticky.' She beams at me, exposing the chipped tooth from a fall several months ago that gives her a vaguely piratical look. I smile back at her, feeling the sunshine on my shoulders. I close my eyes and tip my face up to the light, then sense Grace's shadow appear in front of me. My big girl grins down. She looks entirely relaxed. Her hair is a mess. There is a smudge of ice-cream along her top lip. She looks ten going on twenty-two. Behind her a group of girls call and beckon. I recognise them as classmates from school. Grace plants a kiss on me and then runs back to them. For the next ten minutes they take it in turns to swing on a giant tyre, march laughing along a balance beam and dangle from the climbing frame. When I call that it's time to leave Grace looks reluctant but turns and says goodbye to her friends, and then dashes across to me again, all knees and elbows and breathless enthusiasm.

We have come a long way, Grace and me. She has bloomed under the attention of a special advisory teacher who guided her through a course of sessions about self-esteem. She has learned more about her strengths and weaknesses and emotional resources in a series of meetings with her counsellor. The school now pounces on any instances of bullying and as a result these incidents seem, for now, to have abated. When I collect Grace from school she still comes around the corner alone more often than not, but usually she is smiling. When we go home, she does her homework with fewer groans and often she will go to do her piano practice unasked. Betty will wait patiently by the piano for her big sister to finish, then tug her to the sitting room to play. Smiling, unprotesting, Grace will sit or lie down for Betty to clamber over her in whatever latest game she has devised. When the girls go to bed at night they kiss each other and hug. When I put Grace's light out she wishes me goodnight, and tells me she will love me for ever.

The council have said yes to our request for help. We are now in the next part of the process, in which an assessment is being made of precisely what kind of help Grace needs and how many hours of it a day she requires. This means that the care she has received can continue, alongside some muscular academic training and support tailored to her specific needs. I haven't told her this news but I think Grace senses that things have changed for the better. I am going to bed and sleeping for the first time in months. Next term, when hopefully, barring disaster, we will have confirmation that we have won her a statement of educational needs, we will go again to visit the secondary school we want, this time to show Grace.

A few days later I am back in the office of her primary school and I reflect again how much has changed.

It's early in the morning and from my seat in the waiting area I watch a procession of tiny, scrubbed children pattering past in buttoned-up cardigans and plimsolled toes, a nominee from each class proudly taking the morning register to the school secretary. The air is bright with the start of the day and warm with the scent of baking brownies from the home economics room.

Members of staff pass me and smile warmly. The head-teacher sees me and comes over to say hello and twinkle at me. No longer at odds, we acknowledge each other in the delighted pleasure of success. She thinks Grace's statement will arrive in a matter of weeks now that we have been given the go-ahead for a statutory assessment. It is a relief to lay down arms.

Grace's teacher comes through the door. It is her day off, and she has come in to talk to me about my daughter's progress because I can't make it to next week's parents' evening. Young, beautiful, her hair and skin gleaming, she is all enthusiasm and smiling cheer. She ushers me into an empty room and produces some of Grace's books to show me her work.

We discuss the social situation first: Grace's relationships with the girls in her class and her progress in navigating play-time. She is calmer and more controlled. There are flare-ups with unkind children – school will ever be thus – but to her teacher's and my delight, Grace is holding her own, holding her temper, extracting herself from danger. She has become a good judge of character over the last year's assault course. Now that she can pause and step away from conflict she is able to use that skill to perceive others' motivation and react accordingly. My Aspergers girl is learning.

As her teacher talks to me, she leans towards me and I see her eyes shine. I clutch my handbag tightly and will away the prickle at the back of my own eyes. Grace's teacher tells me how pleased she is that we have secured Grace the support she needs. She tells me how lucky Grace's learning assistant will be to have such a funny and interesting child to work with. She tells me how lovely my daughter is and what a treat it can be to sit beside her and teach her. I swallow hard and

I thank her for all her work and her patience. I tell her this has been a journey for all of us and that I, as much as anyone else, have come a long way in understanding Grace.

At the end of our meeting her teacher produces Grace's creative writing folder. She opens the page at the last exercise, when the class was asked to write a poem about a piece of fruit. This is what Grace has written:

> The watermelon is a green-bottomed boat filled with red
> velvet
> and tiny black people sinking into it.
> The ice-cold taste sends me through happiness
> and the sweet scent works me up into joy.
> The circling shape is like a football. The smoothness
> drops me into a dream.

The teacher and I smile at each other. I want to hug her, but I don't.

Outside, as I walk back to the car, the birds are singing.

If I could only run, the picture would be complete. Instead I am still waiting, biding my time while the deft fingers of my osteopath do their healing work. Meanwhile, I am only allowed to swim. Oh, how I hate swimming. The dip and bob and chlorine gargle as lines of us plough up and down; the tufty-eared old men slowing my pace with their stubborn belief that they should be in the fast lane; the chatting matrons pausing to swap anecdotes at the place where I want to turn. Worse, though, is the feeling of exposure. That moment, that brief wince felt by every female from the age of fourteen, of stepping out on the poolside. The eyes of the men flicking over, pausing slightly too long, then sliding away. I take Grace swimming with me one day and watch her stride alongside me to the water's edge, shoulders back, chin up. Her natural bearing is so confident. I cannot bear to think of it being bowed by male regard.

Now that I can – almost – stop worrying about the school process I realise belatedly that Grace is about to enter another stage for which I must prepare her. She will turn eleven and be a secondary school pupil. She will also turn into a young woman. She is growing up, as those long legs attest, and her angular child's body will soften into curves.

That afternoon as I ploughed up and down on one side of the pool I caught sight of her one moment underwater on the other side, trapped in a shaft of late afternoon sun that pierced to the bottom of the pool. Hair swirling, limbs gracefully arched, absorbed in play, she was utterly divine.

Later, in the shower, we stripped and washed together. Always when I shampoo her hair she puts her arms around me and we hug tightly under the splashing water. She talks to me with her lips against my breastbone, her elbows resting on my hips, entirely unembarrassed by our nakedness. As we dry and dress I see her looking at my body and I wonder what she is thinking. Running has done wonders for my tired post-baby forty-year-old frame. I may be nursing internal injuries for now, but on the outside I look strong and slim. I have lost nearly a stone since the start of this endeavour but I am not submissively skinny. I have muscled thighs and calves; my shoulders and arms are defined. I have learned how to fuel my body for the massive endurance test I will set it: I eat well and often between training sessions and urge my daughter to do the same. This is easy because she hates fizzy drinks and rarely asks for sweets. I hope that her attitudes to body and diet will not change, that she retains her assurance and continues to stand tall, an Amazon in ivory skin. In our house it is the boys who blush and cover and lock the door.

One day in the bathroom she notices my box of tampons and asks about them. I remind her of the talk we had a while ago about periods, and explain. I am brief. She makes a face, says, 'Eeeew' and changes the subject. We have talked about how babies are made – when Betty came along it was impossible not to as Grace wondered daily at the miracle of her creation. She would put an ear to my tummy and sing to her growing sister and marvel that she herself had once fitted in that same space. She sees that my husband and I love each other. She sees us embrace. She comes in to our bedroom in the mornings for a cuddle sometimes to find us curled like spoons. We have bought a bigger bed so that all of our children can fit in it with us on Saturdays. I hope I am teaching Grace about love in a way that lays the foundation for the conversations we must have in the future about sex. How she will cope with puberty and teenage relationships I don't know. Part of me wonders whether in fact she will be streets ahead of her peers, her coping skills battle-hardened after being forged in the heat and fire of primary school turmoil. Part of me knows, though, that there will be more hard lessons ahead.

At least now she has someone to talk to who understands

her life from the inside. Grace is now corresponding by email with another ten-year-old girl who has Aspergers: the daughter of a woman who read my blog and with whom I got chatting online. I hope that Grace and Rebecca can help each other through the rough times. Their messages to each other are an affecting mix of bouncing emoticons and blizzards of exclamation marks, exchanges about the latest film or book or computer game, punctuated by questions like: 'Do you have dyspraxia too?'

There is comfort here for me too, and reassurance in knowing that Rebecca's mother Alice shares some of the same concerns as I do.

'I worry about everything. She's not very good at looking after herself – her personal hygiene isn't very good. If I left her to herself she wouldn't shower, and I have to remind her to change her clothes. So I am dreading her getting her periods. I know that I'll be the one nagging her and reminding her to look after herself,' Alice told me frankly.

Part of our worry is the guesswork about when the onset of puberty will occur, given our daughters' need for consistency. Often the fear of change can be more stressful for them than the change itself, when it comes. As Sophie's mother Nic summed up: 'If you could say to her, "You'll start your period next Tuesday," she'd be fine. It's the uncertainty she gets worked up about.'

With this, as with everything else, the key seems to be prepare, prepare, prepare. I start looking for more reading material, remembering the rollercoaster of my own teenage years and wondering how I would have coped had I been on the spectrum. Adulthood seemed foreign enough as it was, and the expectation that because I was a girl I should also be sexy – despite my boyish frame – was just excruciating. Deciphering boys was impossible. Being friends with them was impossible. Learning the language of swearwords and cool jargon was impossible. To this day, there are times when I wake sweating and mortified to remember the hush that descended on the home economics room when I asked my friend Emma in a too-loud voice: 'What's a twat?' (She told me, bless her, stoically ignoring her own rising blush as the giggles and catcalls grew louder.)

Grace gets on with the boys in her class, by and large, though I think that is because by now she has physically fought several of them and thus earned a grudging respect or distance from them. I wonder whether her direct and matter-of-fact Aspergers brain – the 'male brain' as some scientists term it – will be an advantage to her in relationships, enabling her to bypass emotional bullshit, or whether her difficulty in making friendships will make her vulnerable to young men on the make.

'I worry about boys,' agrees Rebecca as we talk on the phone one night. 'Alice gets on with boys and because she's good she'll often get sat beside a naughty boy in class to be a good influence – so she has developed a soft spot for naughty boys. And because she believes what people say – she takes everything literally – and because she really wants a friend, I worry that she'll put up with bad behaviour from boys. I'm afraid that if a boy tells her they don't need contraception, she'll say, "OK".'

Oh God. I hadn't got that far.

And then, like manna from heaven, a book falls into my lap. Actually, it falls into my Amazon shopping basket, recommended as something other parents have enjoyed. It is a lifesaver. It is called *Aspergirls* and it is written by Rudy Simone, a singer, comic and writer of several books about living with Aspergers. The book is absolutely brilliant. It makes me worry when I read the testimonies of women whose journey into adulthood has been hard. But it tells me clearly what the obstacles may be and it arms me to help my daughter navigate them.

I email Rudy asking if she has time to talk. We chat by Skype, in the end, between London and San Francisco – but minus videolink because Rudy has been out late singing the night before and is feeling 'unkempt', in her words. We start talking and I find I like her immediately: she is funny and direct and sharp. I ask her whether it's harder to go through puberty as a girl with Aspergers or as a boy. She retorts that she hasn't been through puberty as a boy so she can't judge, but then agrees with me that girls face a particular hurdle because they are expected to behave well and look good. 'Girls have to be attractive, to have the right hair, to be witty and charming and socially adept. Whereas if boys are behaving in an incorrect fashion they're just being boys.'

Social situations, Rudy reminds me, are exhausting for people with Aspergers, and for girls coping with the onset of periods and changes to their bodies, the pressure not to do anything that will draw attention or criticism is even higher. 'The slightest thing that can go wrong is multiplied a thousandfold. We often find ourselves in a state of morti-fication – that feeling of "Oh my God, I just did something wrong and it was noticed." For every hour of good social-ising we need another hour's downtime.'

By now I am writing feverish notes to myself. How well our daughters cope with this next stage is largely down to whether they are diagnosed and have the right support. If teachers know and understand, and if parents know and can support them through the emotional upset of adolescence, then they stand a better chance of emerging unscarred at the other end, Rudy tells me.

'Make sure to give her a strong sense that she is a beauti-ful, valid, important individual. Make sure that she isn't withdrawing unless it's for her creative pursuits and that when she is drawing or painting or writing that her solitude is spent happily. Writing saved my life and was my validation. She needs to find her course.'

The next day when we are walking home from school Grace tells me that a friend has been talking about the sec-ondary school he is going to go next, and names one of the local academies. She recounts how the boy asked her if she knew yet where she was going. 'I told him I'd be going to a theatrical school,' she says, 'somewhere I can do art and drama and singing, because that's what I'm good at and it's what I want to do. He said, "Wow, then you'll be going to – "' and she says the name of the school I have held like a hoped-for reward inside my heart these last months. 'So can I go there please, Mummy?' I smile and say I will see what I can do. She tells me that the boy is a good friend. I smile again and pick up her hand, which I am holding, and kiss the back of it. I tell her she is too.

The next day – with just under two weeks to go before the marathon – I see the osteopath, who pronounces me almost cured, and says I can try a short run to see how I get on. Delighted and apprehensive, for this is sooner than I expected to be allowed to try again, I rush home and get changed and start running before I have time to be properly scared. It is unseasonably warm and soon I am sweating in the thick, long-sleeved top and winter running tights that I am wearing. I can feel the injury in my back like a faint bruise and have to force myself to run naturally, suppressing the urge to limp tentatively. After 2 miles I stop and stretch and assess. I feel OK, so I run another 2 miles, this time along the path I first took almost a year ago, past the dog shit and the swings. I can feel my stride loosening and my arms matching the rhythm of my feet. I am breathing hard but it feels good.

I am ready to get back into training. I am ready for the next test.

15

26.2 miles

When I think about Sunday, 22 April, the first thing I think of is the noise: the boom and clamour of the crowd all around, as if I were caught in the centre of a rolling wave that hurled me along and along; the whoosh and thump of my heart behind my eyes and in my ears; the steady one-two-three-four of my breaths, matching my stride; and behind it all a whisper, a murmur behind the din and the hot, roaring pain that came later, a voice that said: Grace, my Grace, my girl.

In the week leading up to the race I managed to keep a lid on my nerves by telling everyone who asked – and there was an increasing number of them as the days passed – that yes, thanks, I was absolutely fine and just aiming to get over the finish line. This was of course entirely untrue: I was not fine, but very scared, and fretting that my injuries and time off training would have badly affected my aim of finishing in under five hours. In the glory days, the flying-down-the-hill-and-laughing days, the early-morning gym squats and muscled weight lifting days of my training, when all was going smoothly and I was getting ever stronger, I had set my sights on a time of four and a half hours, or even slightly less. Now, though my aches and pains were fewer, I was trying to be realistic, albeit less realistic than I pretended to be to everyone who asked.

During this time I had to register my place in the London Marathon, to pick up my runner's number and race chip and kit bag, to sign – in front of a race official – my agreement to participate, to agree that On My Own Head Be It. So I obediently went along as requested to the ExCel conference centre in London's Docklands. Peering through the rain-streaked windows of the train as I arrived, my first impression of it was of an uninspiring cement box with holes for car-parking punched along one side and a stupid name with jarring capital letters emblazoned on a series of signposts. I huffed, and alighted, and walked along the covered walkway to the entrance.

I was not in a good mood. With three days to go before the race, the city was under water: the seam between sky and land a blur of grey wetness. Rain bounced into muddy rivers everywhere as puddles bulged and spread. Cars splashed, bus windows steamed up and commuters' faces took on a pinched, besieged aspect. I thought about ironing my name on to a wetsuit rather than a running vest.

Walking into the hall I removed my hat and shook out my hair and looked up, to be confronted by streams of purposeful people striding out past me. Each carried a red plastic bag with the race sponsorship logo on it. I scanned their faces as each one went by: how would she do on Sunday? And her? And him? Office workers and outdoor types, skinny students and apple-cheeked grandmothers – I gazed at them all, wondering at this carnival of people who would all be pushing along the pavements with me.

Through a red archway was a line of registration kiosks manned by people in branded T-shirts. I took a step forward and trumpets sounded. I started and looked around. Strings soared and swirled. No one else seemed moved. I paused and got my bearings and listened. Music was blasting out from speakers all around me, exuberantly welcoming the arriving runners as they entered the exhibition. I felt a shiver along my scalp, and gulped. Sucker, I told myself. Just go and get your number.

At the kiosk I handed over my passport as identification, and signed a consent form. An old man in glasses presented me with an envelope, explaining which number went on my vest and which on my kit bag. I smiled and thanked him and turned to go, and as I did so he caught my wrist, and patted my hand with papery, arthritic fingers and said: 'Have a good run, love. Have a good fast one.'

Next was a row of people at computer terminals. For a second time my name was checked, this time by a woman who also activated a timing chip and, beckoning me to hand over my bag, sealed it carefully inside before giving it back with a fervent: 'Good luck!'

Blinking, I stumbled along and into the exhibitors' hall, to be faced with a giant wall of colour and scribble, across which giant letters demanded: How will you get through it?

In answer, competitors had inked hundreds of messages on it: good luck wishes and words of love and encouragement spilling across the hoarding. Around us, promotional videos flickered and spun, a blizzard of noise and motion and toned athleticism, exhorting us all to do our best and live the moment while wearing the right brand of sportswear.

I got a glimpse of how Grace must feel sometimes, I think, when trying to process a busy street or noisy classroom, and fled.

In the next room the lines of stalls started in earnest. Tempted to buy a couple of T-shirts and tops, I paused, but then superstition urged me on – what mortification awaited were I to buy official merchandise and then not finish the race. I felt the bruise in my back, the injury like a warning, and walked on.

There were endless stands for clothes and shoes and underwear and sports first aid. One sold only bras, another nothing but injury tape (there were a lot of brave faces in that area). Here was a large, bright stand advertising the Valencia marathon with a video of smiling people loping along in sunshine. Clusters of people stood around to watch it and collect pamphlets. Around the corner the Dublin marathon stand – advertising itself as 'friendly' – was quieter. Around the corner from that, the Munich marathon stand stood empty. A food stand followed, with wall-to-wall power bars, and a drinks stand where confident, good-looking people wore coats marked 'Lucozade Sports Scientists' and approached the crowds with clipboards and a lot of brass neck.

Underneath a sign proclaiming 'I Am Made Of Determination Not Doubt' a worried-looking woman consulted a map and said to her partner: 'There must be a Nike here somewhere.'

Around the next corner I discovered the massage zone – a giant, fenced-off square of groaning rows of prone bodies swathed in towels. Technicians bent over them with busy hands, occasionally revealing a glistening leg or arm or shoulder. The rising fumes of Deep Heat made my eyes prickle and I moved away.

And then it was the end of the exhibition. Another big red arch leading back outside wished us all good luck. At the last minute a man darted out from one of the final stands and asked me: 'Do you want a printout of your body mass index?' Er, no thanks, I told him. He pursued me, and asked: 'Do you want to do some stretching?' Er, I'm ok there too thanks, I told him. He eyed me doubtfully and said, 'Well, OK. Good luck.'

Outside the rain was still pouring and hordes of people were now pushing past me, the trains disgorging hundreds of scurrying figures come to register now the offices were closing and rush hour had started. I stopped and watched and contemplated the race to come and for a moment felt the purest thrill of fear.

Then I remembered how I would get through it, the message I had scribbled on that wall, standing on tiptoes to reach a tiny patch of quiet white space among the tumult of messages, stretching up to print the two words that would keep me putting one foot in front of the other: for Grace.

The night before the marathon I travelled to my sister-in-law's flat, a tiny, twisty fairy-tale garret at the top of an old Victorian house that looked out over south London and the start line, fifteen minutes' journey away. All that day I had been distracted and quick-tempered, pretending to be a participant in Saturday family time while ticking off the hours in my head before it was time to leave. When I could finally go and pack it was a relief, even though, checking and folding my clothes, I felt more as though I was preparing for the executioner's block than the winner's podium. It took an age to pin my running number on to my vest – my hands were shaking so badly that I fumbled the safety pins and pricked my fingers repeatedly.

When I came downstairs to say goodbye to everyone the children stood awkwardly in the doorway, half-turned to run away and play again, half-aware that something was expected from them. A good luck card was produced. I hugged and kissed them all and bent to pick up my kit bag and then Grace was in my arms again. Voice muffled in my chest, she said: 'Do this for me, Mummy.' I held her out from me to look at her face, ready to say something light-hearted and reassuring when, solemnly, she raised three fingers to her lips and held her hand out in salute to me, mimicking the gesture of love and respect used by her new heroine from *The Hunger Games* – the series of books she was currently reading voraciously. It was so Grace: dramatic and funny and sweet and heart-breaking.

That night I slept badly, tossing and turning for hours on the edge of nervous dreams that threatened to throw me into wakefulness. I rose at six, ate porridge and brushed my hair looking in the mirror at my terrified face and listening to the radio, which seemed to be playing in another country – who were these people who could laugh and joke and comment on the lovely weather, preparing for a relaxed day of newspapers and lazy walks and roast dinner?

Outside the sky was clear and the streets largely deserted. I walked down the hill towards the train station alone and in silence, avoiding Saturday-night piles of sick and litter. At a bus stop a woman lit up a cigarette. Then I turned the corner and there were loose knots of people with red race-day kit bags, waiting for the next train. Among them was a friend and fellow runner for the National Autistic Society. The tightness in my stomach loosened.

I don't remember very much about the beginning of the race, except the mass of people around me and in front of me and behind me and the calming voice of my friend, who had done it before, and kept me distracted with stories. Helicopters buzzed overhead and cameras turned on us and the disembodied voice of the race announcer urged us through a tannoy to repeated cheers and whoops as we waited awkwardly, nervously, for the countdown to the start. Then there was a walk, a shuffle, people bouncing on their toes, discarding jumpers and waving goodbye to friends and somehow I'd got to the start line, a huge arch bright red against the blue sky and the pliant mesh of the timing board spongy beneath my shoes, activating the chip tied into my laces, and I was running.

Almost immediately the crowd was there, still modest at this point, strung out like beads along the barrier, sending us good luck and smiles as we set off. We passed an elegant Georgian home in the garden of which two young people on brass instruments puffed out a slightly melancholy version of the *Rocky* theme tune. I found myself pacing behind a purple

Teletubby and in the time it took to puzzle his name – what was it again, was he Po or Tinky Winky? – I realised the first mile was done and I was running the marathon and bobbing along in the centre of a crowd all streaming forward in glorious colour and purpose. For the next few miles we passed several churches that had opened their doors to bless us and cheer us. In front of one, a vicar swung holy water, sending droplets arcing out over the shifting mass, and we raised our hands back, a communal thank you of hundreds. Then there was a choir and a band, and then another band, and then a string of pubs all open, with people dancing on wooden tables outside and waving at us.

So the miles passed. We came to our first incline and as one we all bent, and suffered just a very little bit, and turned to smile with relief at each other as we came over the brow. I found my pace naturally, checking my watch now and again to make sure I wasn't going too fast, or too slow, and finding every time I checked that my body was now automatically doing what I had trained it to do all those months and was carrying me forward with ease. A bit of me floated away and just watched the carnival around me as I progressed. Then the route turned right, and we all turned right and suddenly in front of us was Tower Bridge and I'd run twelve and a half miles and was passing under the grey turrets and the crowd was going crazy. Down along the highway the crowds were deeper and deeper – three or four back from the barriers and screaming and shouting. It was a huge effort not to speed up, for I was loving every moment, grinning like a loony, knowing that my family were going to appear at any moment at mile fourteen, where the National Autistic Society had organised a cheering point. I ran with my neck craned, seeking out the purple and white and red balloons and banners and feeling goosebumps running up along the back of my neck in anticipation. And then there they were – only on the other side of the barrier where I couldn't touch them – so I yelled and jumped up and down, pumping my arms in victory and blowing kisses and the roar that went up was for me, for me and for Grace and for us all and as I ran away I was overcome and saw the route ahead of me blurred for a while.

When I came to again it was mile fifteen and something wasn't right. Before I had time to figure out what was bothering me I felt a hand on my shoulder, the runner behind me directing me to a voice in the crowd to my left. It was my friend and former running partner Karen, who had started with me nearly a year ago, puffing and blowing and swapping stupid jokes with me on those first training runs as I contemplated my first half-marathon. I shrieked with joy and ran to her and she grabbed me. Both of us wild-eyed and teary, we exchanged kisses and loving words – none of which I can remember now – and then I was running again, careering forward in a state of such massive emotion that I'm amazed, thinking of it now, that I didn't spontaneously combust on the spot.

By sixteen and a half miles I'd worked out what wasn't right. The pain in my back had bloomed again, despite those weeks of enforced rest and expert osteopath attention, and the first corresponding shivers of pain were sending feelers down my right leg. A swooping downward lurch of panic hit me. I tried to shake it off and keep going but the pain was building very quickly and with it, my distress.

So I did what you do when the going gets tough and the tough need to get going: I went for a wee and a think, veering off the course to where a line of portaloos stood and barricading myself inside one to shut in my panic. There, in the dim blue light and the animal smell of other people's fear, I chewed painkillers and took shaky breaths and thought: how do I do this, how do I get going again. The murmur told me: Grace.

So I came out and I started running again, only I couldn't. I told myself I would walk half a mile and then try again. I counted down to seventeen and a half miles and started running again. But the pain built up anew, so I walked and hobbled, pushing out thoughts of failure and ashamedly hoping that no one would see me walking, and then I forced myself to run again. By now I'd passed the 18-mile mark and there again was Karen, yelling at me from the barricades. Sagging with relief and self-pity I went to her and fastened myself around her neck and told her, choked, how much it hurt. She hugged me back tightly and told me how well I was doing. Around us the crowd looked at our embrace and looked at my face. Arms came out and patted me and told me I could do it. A blur of faces pushed into mine and said, come on, come on. Karen released me back into the flow of runners and I found my pace and ran again.

The next 3 miles were misery. At this point the route had taken us into the heart of Canary Wharf, all hard-faced glittering windows and no progress: we wound around and around, marking time and miles until we could turn back towards the centre of town and the final stretch. But not yet, and not yet, and not yet. We passed restaurants and wine bars and offices – including my own place of work, an incentive to run straighter and a bit faster, no matter how much it hurt – and here the crowds shouted for Toby and Robert, and yelled, 'Come on, old man!' and bellowed rugby shouts of 'Whoooooarrrrrgh!' for confident, young specimens who strode out and overtook all around me.

Then, thank God, we were released, leaving the glistening maze behind us and heading back out towards my family and friends and the NAS crowd of supporters who I knew were all waiting at mile twenty-one, scanning the crowd anxiously, their gazes turned so far out into the mass as they searched for me that they jumped when I came up the inside lane and whooped in their faces. Ecstatic, I did a little dance and they laughed, and grabbed me. My parents and sisters, tears in their eyes, clutched me. My husband leaned forward for a kiss and Betty and the boys – hot and sticky – smiled and put their hands out to me. And there was Grace, smiling and kissing me and asking me: 'Why are you crying?'

At that point I thought I'd done it. Leaving everyone I loved behind me with a wave and a promise to see them at the finish, I thought I'd cracked it. I ran on, back along the highway – the roar from the crowd building to an astonishing pitch – and into Blackfriars tunnel and an incline to the Victoria Embankment. As I bent into it the pain in my back came over me in a huge wave. For a panic-stricken moment I thought that I was going to be sick or black out. Breathing, concentrating, I emerged from the tunnel sandwiched in the middle of the staggering pack, to an immense mass of people screaming encouragement. A sign told me I had only two and a half miles to go. Around me I could see runners smiling through their exhaustion and managing a final spurt. But all I could manage was a hobble, a limping half-walk, and then a walk – biting my lips not to cry in front of all these people. My watch showed that I still had twenty minutes before five hours had passed. I walked as quickly as I could bear to, hoping to ease out the pain enough to pick up a run again, and started a distracted, frayed conversation with a similarly wrung-out runner alongside me.

At the corner of Big Ben I turned and saw, if it were possible, an even bigger crowd. I started running again, unable to bear the humiliation of walking in front of so many, despite being almost cross-eyed with pain. The route turned into St James Park and along Birdcage Walk, and while my mind was yelling at me to stop, it was also registering dimly that this was nearly the end. A sign said 800 metres and I nearly threw myself down on the floor at the thought of how far I still had to go. But then I turned and there was Buckingham Palace and the Mall and people were ten deep at the barricades, hanging off lampposts and thronged, waving, in the fountains and there was no way I could stop in front of them all, so I plodded on, weaving and bent, and there in front of me was another red arch like the one I had gone through nearly five hours ago. The clock on top of it said four hours and fifty-four minutes. I headed for it and was aware that I was smiling, that we were all smiling, and that it was nearly the end.

I crossed the finish line two minutes later and raised my

arms intending to make a victory gesture but found instead, as I slowed to a final stop, that I was clutching my head and weeping. Wiping my face with sticky hands, I followed lines of shattered runners submitting to the attentions and directions of race officials. A young man removed my time chip from my shoes while a woman strung a medal around my neck. In a daze, I collected my kit bag, slung it over my shoulder and started out into the crowds again to find my daughter.

It took an age. By now the crowds on the Mall were apocalyptic: huge and growing ever bigger as more and more runners came through and their families pushed forward to meet them. Parts of the mass were blocked solid, unmoving, and threaded with panic as some people began to realise they were trapped. I stood for a short while among them, tearing into the food and drink that had been offered to me in my finisher's pack, swallowing and drinking and assessing the scene in front of me. In the end I pushed sideways, scrabbling over the metal barriers with legs and back screaming in protest, and falling through into the park, where I stumbled on to where I was supposed to meet my family, by the NAS banner, scanning all the time for Grace.

No one was there but several volunteer staff, who stepped forward instantly to relieve me of my kit bags and put a coat around me. The sky had turned overcast and a wind was getting up. Gently, they set aside my protests that I had to wait for my family, telling me they'd take care of it, and put me in the care of someone who steered me along a further ten-minute walk to a white-terraced building on Whitehall that was the venue for the society's after-party, where showers and hot food and massages were provided. I tottered along worried and fatigued, following another NAS runner who'd joined us. At one point she turned to me and asked me my time. I told her – four minutes under five hours – and she nodded and told me hers, a full half an hour faster than me. Something woke then and a voice popped up inside my head and said: 'I bet you could do it faster next year.' I blinked and it was gone, but for an echo.

Once inside the building, I was ushered to a comfortable room with a shower and told I had fifteen minutes. It took me five to undo my shoelaces and a further five to remove my shoes. I hobbled back to the door and opened it to ask if I could please have my fifteen minutes from now. The staff looked at me – dishevelled, sweaty, with salt streaks down the sides of my face and the line of my hat still banded across my forehead – and took pity and said yes.

When I re-emerged, clean, into the foyer, everyone had arrived. Betty bolted for me, clutching me around the knees so that I staggered and nearly fell, and then there was Grace at last. Grinning, hopping, her eyes huge against a tangle of dark hair, she grabbed me and waltzed with me for a moment, shouting to me: 'Congratulations, Mummy!' among the hubbub as the rest of my family absorbed me into a group embrace. In their arms I finally let go of the last scrap of energy that was keeping me upright and slid, gracelessly, to the floor, laughing and crying all at once. Grace knelt beside me and put her arm around my neck and her ears to my mouth and breathed: 'Hey, guess what,

Mummy, I've walked *miles* today. Do you want to see my blisters?'

Much later, after the celebrations and the victory meal and the long-awaited champagne, I finally fell into bed. But that night and for the rest of the week I barely slept, passing instead into an over-exhausted, jittery trance where I replayed Sunday's events over and over in my head. I felt a huge sense of achievement but also a sense of waiting, as though the final judgment had somehow been withheld.

By now the Easter holidays had passed and Grace was back at school, in the diurnal round of classroom learning and play and homework and clubs that not so long ago had caused her so much distress. Watching her from the strangely distant place in which I found myself, she seemed barely recognisable as the child I had started to write about so many months before. Smiling and calm as I greeted her in the playground, she would come home and bow obediently over her homework then she and Betty would go and lark about in their bedrooms until I called them for dinner. She read, drew, watched television, and talked cheerfully about the games she'd played with friends at school. She'd sneak downstairs when she should have been sleeping, to ask for one last, extra cuddle on the sofa. There, occasionally, she would recount a scuffle or two at school, minor incidents for which she sought advice. But that wrinkle of worry in her forehead, the shade of pale anxiety in her cheek, was gone.

The weekend after the marathon, I put on some music in the sitting room and danced with my husband for the first time in a long time.

'I think I'm ok again,' I told him. 'I think I'm back.'

He smiled and pulled me closer.

On 30 April, the ballot opened for places in the 2013 London Marathon.

I put my name down.

Appendix

The point of you

Grace, sweetheart, listen because I think I know what the point of you is.

One per cent of the population are spectrum folk. That means that you probably don't know all that many yet, but there are a lot. There are 62,300,000 people in the UK. So that means 623,000 are on the spectrum. Most of these people have not yet discovered their Aspieness. For example, I'm a 33-year old Aspie and Aspergers wasn't even known about when I was at school. They're getting better at spotting Aspie kids now, but adults who are doing really well and achieving lots aren't anywhere in the statistics because no-one has ever spotted them. This generally means that all people know about are the Aspie adults with the worst mental health problems and the most severe autism. The likes of you and me don't tend to be known about at all. This causes some problems, for example, everyone (me included) tends to overreact when they get a diagnosis and imagine that things are far worse than they actually are. Also, now, when I tell people I'm an Aspie, if they know anything about the spectrum, they tend to assume that I cannot do stuff. They are staggered and amazed that I live independently from my parents, in my own flat. When I then tell them I used to be a type of lawyer and that I have paid off my mortgage, they then look like they are going to fall off their chairs. The point is, that no-one has quite understood the likes of you and me yet. The professionals get some bits right, but other bits, they can get really wrong.

In a way, I was quite lucky because I didn't know that I was an Aspie until age 29. Not that there is anything wrong with being an Aspie or knowing about it. But I was protected, at least, for a long time from other people's mistaken beliefs that we are not very capable. Don't get side-tracked by any of these wrong beliefs. It's really important that you keep believing in yourself and how incredibly capable you are. Don't let anyone tell you that you cannot do anything because of being an Aspie. It's not true. Some things will be harder than for other people, but nothing is impossible. Also, some other things will be much easier for you than for other people. For example, things that are much easier for me than most people include having perfect pitch, music, French and maths. Your gifts might not be exactly the same as mine. But there will be things that you can do incredibly easily that other people would find really hard.

Some super-wonderful things about you are: you are very, very bright. Half of people on the spectrum never learn to talk and lots have a learning disability. This means that you will be able to think your way around problems that others might think would be impossible for you.

You will be a great communicator. Sounds impossible? Communication is one of the 'triad of impairments' – yeuch, what a horror of a term – really, these words can be pretty harmful and they are only used because the people who first discovered and wrote about the autistic spectrum are non-spectrum psychologists and not Aspies. But I can tell you it isn't impossible to be an Aspie and a good communicator because people tell me that I am a fantastic communicator. Because you are so very, very clever, you will be able to find ways around the things that are extra-difficult for you.

You are able to trust – you trust your mum enough to tell her what's happening in your life. That is so fantastic, sweetheart. This is such a good strategy for life. Never bottle anything up. I will learn this from you.

You are absolutely gorgeous – I've seen your picture on the blog.

You are able to love. I'm only just learning this bit now, so you are years and years ahead of me, emotionally, already.

You are creative – you dance, sing, act and dress up.

You're funny. This is a very attractive quality and will win you friends.

You are so, so brave. You don't give up. This is incredibly important. You tell the truth. This is a lovely quality and people value you for this.

You give great hugs and kisses. I'm only just learning how to do this. Again, you are years ahead of me. And other people will love you for it, your whole life long.

Appendix: The point of you

You encourage other people – you told someone that you liked their drawing. This is fantastic. Everyone needs encouragement, and most British people tend to be incredibly bad at giving it. Aspies find it really difficult to know how other people think and feel, but we can be fantastic at encouraging others, supporting and affirming them.

You are not limited in your choices to what the world sees as 'normal'. This is a really valuable trait to have. It gives you a lot of wiggle-room to choose what is right for you.

You stick up for yourself. Again, you are way ahead of me in this because I have never managed to do that. It is really hard to control all of our emotions, because we feel all of them a bit more strongly than non-spectrum folk do. I'm not saying that lashing out at people is a great strategy and it's a good plan to listen to your mum and do your best to control yourself. But there is always an upside to these things, and the upside of this is that you are no-one's doormat. Probably my usual way of locking everything inside is far worse.

You are not a bad person because you get angry. Everyone gets angry. It's a natural emotion. It's a useful emotion. If someone kicked me in the face, then the right emotional response is to feel anger. It would be a bit stupid to feel pleased about it, and anyone who felt like this would not live very long. So, it's completely right to feel angry – just try to find a way to express it that doesn't hurt other people. Try your best to control your anger. But if that doesn't work out, you are still not a bad person if you have done your best. You don't do anything for no reason. It's only because you are getting provoked beyond the point that anyone could possibly bear. This does not make you bad. Just do your best – it's all that any of us can do, and it's all that anyone can ask of you.

You have a great destiny. Those 623,000 people in the UK who are on the spectrum – they need YOUR help. They will see you succeeding and being a great example and role model for them. They need your encouragement, your wisdom and your love. They need you to be a voice and speak up for them. They need you to tell the world things that they cannot tell it, because of their communication difficulties. They need to know your coping strategies. And there is a whole load of other people who need you to explain what it's like to be an Aspie to them, because they don't get it. Even many of the professionals don't get it. They need you to explain things to them from your point of view. And they will be fascinated. They will think you are incredible. They will go away thinking: 'Wow, I've never met anyone like Grace before, she's so inspirational, she has completely changed my idea of what the autistic spectrum is'.

You will change people's lives. This is a great destiny. And no idiot of a nine-year-old boy is going to keep you from that. It's not possible. This is also a destiny that would be impossible if you were not an Aspie. I've written a book. But if I was the same as everyone else, I could not have written my book, and no-one would be interested in reading it.

You will be able to help and encourage Aspies of all ages. When you are older, you will be great at playing with children, Aspies or otherwise. Aspies always know what it is like to be a child, but it is something that other people seem to forget when they grow up. In many ways, Aspies have a lot more fun than everyone else. Non-Aspies are really worried, all the time, about what other people think of them, and it really restrains their behaviour and makes their lives a lot less fun than they could be. We don't have this problem. In some ways, I think other people would like to be more like me, but they're not brave enough.

You will be great at teaching and explaining things to other people. Aspies are great at communication and we are fabulously clear and coherent. This is a fantastic skill when it comes to talking to children, to people with autism and to non-native English language speakers. I can often explain things to people in the right way, whilst other people make the mistake of talking in a too complicated style.

Our uniqueness is something that I can give to people – I've only just discovered this. And some people really like it. Most people don't understand us very well, but some people will just 'get us' and it's fantastic that such people exist.

Also, it is really, really hard being an Aspie sometimes. But there is often a way to turn our bad experiences into something good. When people misunderstood me and got angry at me for something that I didn't intend, I wrote these things down in my book, to explain my point of view and help everyone reading it to understand better. When I had some other bad experiences, I found out how to get healed, emotionally, and then wrote a guide book to help other Aspies avoid the mistakes that I had made, so that they will understand better and be safer than I was. When I meet another Aspie who has been bullied, I know how she feels because it has happened to me, and so I can empathise. It feels so often like we are on our own and this is all just happening to us. But we are not alone, ever. You will be able to turn some of your bad experiences into something really good and worthwhile.

Another thing – just because other people say something doesn't mean it is true. Even if a lot of people say it. Some people lie for their own reasons. Many people who feel insecure about themselves (and who feel broken and hurt inside) look for someone else to pick on, just to make themselves feel better. This is really wrong and should never happen, but it does. Other people just make mistakes and don't take the time and effort to properly understand – they leap to the wrong conclusion.

Here is an example of lots of people saying and thinking something that was not true. A long time ago, everyone thought that the sun went around the earth. In fact, a man called Galileo worked out that it is the other way around – the earth goes around the sun. Everyone told Galileo that he was wrong. But Galileo was right and everyone else was wrong. I don't care how many people tell you that you are mean. They are just as wrong as everyone who thought the sun went around the earth, and you are not, not, NOT under any circumstances to believe this. You are a lovely, sweet, brave, brave girl who has just been pushed too far beyond what any human being could reasonably bear. This is not the same as being mean. You are not guilty. Not guilty. No arguing. This is the truth.

I've now met a lot of Aspies. Some of them have a lot of difficulty controlling their anger. But I don't think I actually have met any Aspie who is mean. We simply aren't mean people. We are some of the nicest people on earth. There are plenty of good things about being an Aspie, and this is one of them. Lots of non-spectrum people try to manipulate others for their personal gain. Aspies don't do this. It's not in our nature. Bullies are mean because they hurt people intentionally, for no reason. That is the definition of mean. You are not mean.

Precious one, you are simply fantastic and you have a wonderful future ahead of you. You are more capable and more lovely than you can possibly know.

Lots of love,

Debi xxx

Acknowledgements and disclaimers

While this book was written during my employment as a Reuters journalist, Reuters has not been involved with the content or tone of this book, which is my responsibility alone.

There are very many people I'd like to thank, not least the online community of friends and supporters who read my blog and sent me compliments and encouragement as well as generous donations, and helped me believe that I could keep going.

In particular I send a big thank you to my running partner Karen, who carried me along in all senses, and to my colleague and dear chum Kate, who set the bar (and who I hope will be running those lovely 9-milers again soon) and to Catherine Mayer, a wonderful mentor and inspirational writer and friend.

To all the parents who contributed to this book and who accompanied me on this marathon, to those who keep on keeping on and who showed me that it can be done – I can never adequately express my gratitude and admiration for you all.

To all the staff at the National Autistic Society, in particular the anonymous lady at the end of the telephone line that night, who picked me up and dusted me off; and to Jenny, Cecilia and Beth, heartfelt thanks for your help with everything.

None of this would have happened without my agent Clare Hulton, to whom I am forever grateful for inviting me to the dance, and to all the staff at Piatkus – particularly Anne Lawrance and Zoe Goodkin – who were such marvellous partners. Thanks especially to my patient, deft editor Anne Newman and to Sophie Burdess who created this book's lovely cover.

Finally, I want to thank my family for their love and support throughout all the ups and downs. My mum and dad for reading early drafts and helping me to find my voice again, and my sisters Cathy and Harry for holding me tight and not minding that so much of the conversation was about me. The father of our special girl, who knows more than anyone what a wonder we made. And to Mike McCarthy, godfather of joy, who got me started on this writing lark when I was ten years old – thank you.

And last, but never least, to Chris: team-mate, coach and cheerleader. I love you.

Useful resources

The National Autistic Society
Always the first port of call, for information, advice, counselling, support, further resources and details of local communities and networks:
Address: The National Autistic Society
　　　　393 City Road
　　　　London
　　　　EC1V 1NG
Tel: +44 (0)20 78332299
Email: nas@nas.org.uk
Website: www.autism.org.uk
Facebook page: www.facebook.com/NationalAutisticSociety
Autism Helpline: 0808 800 4104 (lines are open 10 a.m.–4 p.m. Monday to Friday)

IPSEA (Independent Parental Special Education Advice)
For advice on navigating the school system, in particular how to get additional support and a statement of education needs, as well as appealing and tribunals:
General Advice Line: 0800 018 4016

Tribunal Help Line: 0845 602 9579
Facebook page: www.facebook.com/ipsea.page

Online resources
Advice, chat and resources for people who have Aspergers:
www.wrongplanet.net
www.neurodiversity.com/main.html

For parents and carers seeking others in the same situation;
advice, chat forums, resources:
www.mumsnet.com/special-needs

Via Facebook:
www.facebook.com/aspergersawarenesspage
www.facebook.com/pages/Parenting-Aspergers-Children-Support-Group/101589699900722
www.facebook.com/AutismWomensNetwork

For help coping with bullying:
Beat Bullying: www.beatbullying.org
Kidscape: www.kidscape.org.uk
Childline: www.childline.org.uk or 0800 1111

Recommended reading

The National Autistic Society has a very comprehensive list of books on its website, but here are some that Grace and I liked in particular:

The Complete Guide To Asperger's Syndrome by Tony Attwood (Jessica Kingsley, 2008)

Aspergirls: Empowering Females with Asperger Syndrome by Rudy Simone (Jessica Kingsley, 2010)

Can I Tell You About Asperger Syndrome? A Guide for Friends and Family by Jude Welton (Jessica Kingsley, 2003)

Martian in the Playground: Understanding the Schoolchild with Asperger's Syndrome by Clare Sainsbury (Sage Publications, 2009)

Raising Martians – From Crash-Landing to Leaving Home: How to Help a Child with Asperger's Syndrome or High-Functioning Autism by Joshua Muggleton (Jessica Kingsley, 2011)

Freaks, Geeks and Asperger Syndrome: A User Guide to Adolescence by Luke Jackson (Jessica Kingsley, 2002)

Different Like Me: My Book of Autism Heroes by Jennifer Elder (Jessica Kingsley, 2005)

All Cats Have Asperger's Syndrome by Kathy Hoopmann (Jessica Kingsley, 2006)